DAVID EDGAR with Susan Todd

Teendreams

DAVID EDGAR

Our Own People

A Methuen Paperback

A METHUEN MODERN PLAY

This collection first published in Great Britain in 1987 by Methuen
London Ltd, 11 New Fetter Lane, London EC4P 4EE and in the
United States of America by Methuen Inc., 29 West 35th Street,
New York, NY 10001
This collection copyright © 1987 by David Edgar.

Teendreams first published in Methuen New Theatrescripts in 1979
by Eyre Methuen Ltd.
Copyright © 1979 by David Edgar and Susan Todd
Fully revised and reprinted in this edition for Methuen Modern Plays
Copyright © 1987 by David Edgar and Susan Todd

Our Own People first published by Methuen London Ltd in 1987
Copyright © 1987 by David Edgar

Printed and bound in Great Britain by
Richard Clay Ltd, Bungay, Suffolk

British Library Cataloguing in Publication Data

Edgar, David
  Teendreams; &, Our own people.——
  (Methuen modern plays).
  I. Title II. Edgar, David. Our own people
  822'.914   PR6055.D44

ISBN 0 413 16890 5

CAUTION
This play is fully protected by copyright. All enquiries concerning
the rights for professional or amateur stage productions should be
addressed to Michael Imison Playwrights Ltd, 28 Almeida Street,
London N1; Abbe Levin, 105 West 70th Street, No. IR, New
York, N.Y. 10023; or Virginia Ferguson, 98-106 Kippax Street,
Surrey Hills, Sydney, N.S.W. 2010.

To Eve

CONTENTS

Teendreams

Monstrous Regiment was formed in 1975 as a touring theatre company with a majority of women members, whose work was intended to explore the experience of women past and present, placing that experience in the centre of the stage, instead of in the wings.

Teendreams was the company's sixth production and its first venture into working with a male writer. The form of the work was, initially, a discussion of possible themes between David Edgar and Susan Todd as collaborators. The company then undertook a workshop/discussion period which included sessions with women who had special areas of expertise (including Angela McRobbie, Liz Whitman, Beatrix Campbell and Eve Brook). The content, form, structure and progression of the play was then assembled by David and Susan into a detailed synopsis, which was then discussed by the whole company. David then wrote the play from the sum of this work.

Teendreams began its first tour in Bristol in January 1979. Eight years later, the opportunity arose to rework the play for a production by drama students in the same city. The text in this book emerged from considerable work between the authors, director Martin White and the Bristol University Drama Department Third Year performance group in early 1987.

Teendreams was first presented by the Monstrous Regiment at the Van Dyck Theatre, Bristol, on 25 January 1979, with the following cast:

TRISHA/CATHY/SANDRA	Chris Bowler
FRANCES	Gillian Hanna
ROSIE/DEBBIE	Susan Todd
RUTH/SHARON/LYNNE	Jenifer Armitage
DAVE/HOWARD/TONY/BREWER	Clive Russell
COLIN/KEVIN/GARY	David Bradford
ANNE/MARIA/DENISE	Mary McCusker

Directed by Kate Crutchley
Designed by Di Seymour
Lighting by Meri Jenkins

The revised version of the play was first presented by the Department of Drama of Bristol University in the same theatre, on 11 March 1987, with the following cast:

TRISHA/CATHY/ANNE	Julia Selby
FRANCES	Justine Midda
ROSIE/DEBBIE	Sara Fleming
KEVIN/COLIN/GARY	Tim Dynevor
HOWARD/DAVE/TONY/BREWER	Mark Ravenhill
RUTH/SHARON	Alexandra Saint
SANDRA/DENISE	Colette Wrigley

Directed by Martin White
Assisted by Dot Peryer
Set Design by Jennie Norman
Stage Managed by Juliet Fox

The play is set in England. The main action takes place in 1975, with flashbacks to 1968, 1972 and 1961.

Scene One

Music: 'Will You Still Love Me Tomorrow' by the Shirelles.

FRANCES' *flat, summer 1975. A sofa, in front of it a coffee table. On the table a big 60s political poster book. Nearby a record-player and tape-deck. A glass of whisky on the same table.*

TRISHA, *who's 15 and dressed in an approximate school uniform, sits on the sofa. A moment. Then she leans forward, as if to open the book. But* FRANCES *enters, and* TRISHA *recoils.* FRANCES *is 26, dressed at present in a T-shirt and jeans.*

FRANCES. Well, hallo there, Trisha.

TRISHA. 'Lo, miss.

FRANCES. Oh, heavens. Frances, please.

She goes out the other side. ROSIE *enters after a moment, from the same side. She's the same age as* FRANCES, *but dolled up. She smiles at* TRISHA *and goes out the other side. Pause.* TRISHA *reaches for the book again, but again is interrupted by* FRANCES, *who enters buttoning a blouse.*

FRANCES. Now, do please make free with the kitchen. And there's the record player and some stuff on tape.

(*As she goes*). Doubt if they'll be to your taste. All classical and golden oldies, I'm afraid.

She goes out. Once again, ROSIE *crosses the stage in the opposite direction. Then* FRANCES *re-enters, zipping her evening trousers.*

FRANCES. Hey, wasn't it your last?

TRISHA. Beg pardon?

FRANCES. Last exam.

TRISHA. Oh, yuh.

FRANCES. So, how d'you do?

TRISHA *shrugs.*

TRISHA (*doubtfully*). OK.

FRANCES. OK.

She goes. Pause. This time, TRISHA *has time to open the book.* ROSIE *enters as* TRISHA *reads.*

ROSIE. Dead to the world.

She switches off the tape. Cut the Shirelles.

TRISHA. Uh – sorry?

ROSIE. Kids.

TRISHA. Oh, good.

ROSIE. Dead right. What's this?

TRISHA *shows her the book.* ROSIE *reads:*

'Wherever death may surprise us, let it be welcome, provided that this, our battle cry, may have reached some receptive ear, and another hand may be extended to wield our weapons, and other men be ready to intone the funeral dirge with the staccato chant of the machine gun and new battle cries of war and victory'. Phew.

FRANCES *has entered. She carries a mac.*

FRANCES. It's Che Guevara.

Slight pause.

Murdered by the forces of reaction in the jungles of Bolivia when you were six. Or seven.

Slight pause.

Is there anything, damper, than yesterday's dreams?

Pause.

ROSIE. So, are we ready?

FRANCES. Yup.

ROSIE. Their names are Damion and Sophie.

FRANCES (*gives a piece of paper to* TRISHA): Here's the number where we'll be.

ROSIE. So, then. By bye.

FRANCES (*As they go, with her mac*): I decided that it looked like rain.

FRANCES *and* ROSIE *go.* TRISHA *puts down the book. Pause. She stands, goes to the tape deck and puts on the tape. It's Julie Driscoll, 'This Wheel's on Fire'.* TRISHA *stops and fast forwards and plays. It's Grace Slick, 'White Rabbit'.* TRISHA *stops, fast forwards and plays. It's Suzi Quatro, 'Your Momma Won't Like Me'.* TRISHA *lets this play a little, but it clearly distresses her. Then she stops it. She puts on the record player. The record on the turntable is Carole King's 'It Might As Well Rain Until September'. She plays it from the beginning.*

TRISHA *picks up the whisky, and takes it to the sofa. She sits, takes out a bottle of pills. She starts to take the pills, washed down by the whisky. The music swells.*

Fade to blackout.

Scene Two

FRANCES' *flat. A day or two later. The poster book is shut on the table.* FRANCES *sits on the sofa. A suitcase is nearby.* ROSIE *stands near her.*

FRANCES. You know, when *I* was 15, I remember, was the same as poor old Trisha. Yes, I used to think, like she did, when I met him at the candy store, and when he whispered sweet and secret nothings in my ear, and when we walked off hand in hand into the sunset, that in that very moment, suddenly my whole life changed. But, still, the thing was, I did know, p'raps unlike Trisha, deep down, that the whole shebang was so much shit. It wouldn't last. The blissful moment was, by definition, just momentary.

But when I was 19, and went to college, 1968, the dawn in which of course 'twas bliss to be alive, and when I met him at the demo and he whispered sweet and secret dialectics in my ear, and when we walked off hand in hand into the sit-in, and in *that* very moment suddenly my whole life changed . . .

I thought it had.

And, even more, I thought *that* tatty teenage fantasy was going to be a blueprint for the Changing of the World.

You know?

It's simple. Thought we could change people.

We were wrong.

And so, friend Rosie, I am going home.

ROSIE. Frances. Don't go.

FRANCES stands and goes to her suitcase.

FRANCES. Back home. Where I'll be safe.

ROSIE. Stay here. At least a day or two.

FRANCES picks up her case.

FRANCES. Returning back, where I belong. Back to the past. Because I liked it there.

She remembers she's forgotten something. She snaps her fingers. Puts down her case, goes out.

ROSIE. Speak for yourself. Friend Frances.

Lights fade to a spot on ROSIE.

Scene Three

As the scene changes, play the Wedding March and bells. Hold the spot on ROSIE, fade up spots on HOWARD and KEVIN. ROSIE is watching, respectively, her husband and his best man, at her wedding in 1968.

Fade music.

KEVIN. Right then, first of all thanks to the bridesmaids and the pageboy, Tracy leave Lee alone, I always said little girls should be obscene and not heard.

Never tell an Irishman a joke on Saturday in case he laughs in church.

Howard, wanted by the police. Mum says, no accounting for taste.

Howard, if all the birds he's had laid end to end, I wouldn't be at all surprised.

Sorry Rosie, had to slip it in. As the Art Mistress said to the postman. Speaking of which.

He unfolds a telegram.

First telegram. 'Note merged accounts stop future products filed in pending query hope not triplicate congrats from all at office'.

Filed in pending. Triplicate. It's the way I tell 'em.

Number two. 'The Students' Union'. 'The University'. To Rosie. 'Dont' – I s'pose that's 'Don't', 'don't forget your promises love Frances'. Well.

You tell em, gel. Reality is just an escape for people who can't cope with drugs.

Well, onward to the revolution. Next –

Snap blackout on KEVIN *and* HOWARD.
We see FRANCES, *dressed as she will be in the next scene, watching* ROSIE. *Darkness.*

Scene Four

Music: 'Those Were the Days' by Mary Hopkin.

It is broken into by a metallic TANNOY, *over the hubbub of many voices.*

During the TANNOY, *fade up lights on the scene.*

It is the summer of 1968. We are in the corner of a Victorian-Gothic University Hall, which is presently under occupation. A few sleeping-bags lie around.

Left, a table, at which a student, RUTH, *is typing a leaflet on a stencil.*

Centre, and facing upstage, is the kneeling CATHY, *who is making placards with a red magic-marker on pieces of card. She has already completed two, which read:*

'Don't Demand – Occupy' and 'Revolution is the Festival of the Oppressed'.

CATHY *wears a short skirt.*

TANNOY. Well, good morning, campers, this is your friendly neighbourhood occupation organising committee, and first of all, for any new occupants, breakfast of a sort is being served in the Registry reception, recently acquisitioned for the people – oh and agitprop wants to know, if anyone can work a Gestetner could they go to the agitprop desk which I believe is situated in the Bursary like pronto. Thank you and have just a wonderful day.

The hubbub fades up again. CATHY *picks up her third placard. It reads: 'Death to the Plastic Culture'.*

CATHY. Hey. Ruth.

RUTH (*not looking round*). Mm?

CATHY. Hey, Ruth, you suppose this is all right?

RUTH turns and looks.

RUTH. Lovely. What's it mean?

CATHY reads her placard.

CATHY. Well now, there I think you have me.

RUTH back to typing.
CATHY checks a list and starts work on another placard.
Enter DAVE, a student leader, wearing a red armband and carrying papers. He strides over to RUTH.

DAVE. Colin?

RUTH. I'm sorry?

DAVE. Where's bloody Colin.

RUTH. I don't know, Dave. Ask Frankie.

DAVE. Where is Frankie?

RUTH. Dunno, Dave. She's been around.

DAVE (*glances at his watch*). That's great.

He drums his fingers.
Then, for something else to do, he reads the top of the stencil RUTH is typing.

What's this for?

RUTH. It's a leaflet, Dave.

DAVE. Oh, yuh?

RUTH. What d'you think of it?

DAVE. Yuh, well . . .

He looks round, vaguely.
Sees CATHY at her work and looks at her short skirt.

Yuh, well, at this precise moment I'm not that concerned with the politics of the transitional programme in late monopoly capitalism. Like at this precise juncture I'm a bit more bothered about why the Halls of Residence weren't leafleted, what's up with the Gestetner and why we appear to be minus one bloody hero.

To RUTH:

If you see what I mean.

RUTH. Oh, sure.

DAVE decides to go. He passes CATHY *and glances at her skirt and then her work.*

DAVE. Hey, Cath.

CATHY (*kneels up*). Yes? What?

DAVE. Two 'C's' in 'consciousness'.

CATHY. I see.

FRANCES has entered left. DAVE *notices.*

DAVE. Ah. Frankie.

FRANCES. Yes.

DAVE. You know if Colin's coming in?

FRANCES. I think so.

DAVE. Think so.

FRANCES. Well, he said –

She's interrupted by the TANNOY.

TANNOY. 'Tention Comrade Robertson. Please go to the admin desk. Comrade D. Robertson to the admin desk. Oh, sorry, scrub that, Dave, I mean the Soc Soc desk.

DAVE. I try to run a revolution.

DAVE goes out.
CATHY is looking at her finished placard. It reads: 'Freedom is the Consciousness of our Desires'. The second 'c' of 'consciousness' is inserted.

CATHY. Well, that'll have to do.

To FRANCES:

Well, will he speak?

She gets up, collects up her placards.
During the following, unnoticed, COLIN *enters. He is 20, dressed with informal elegance, and a sense of the drama of the events about to take place.*

FRANCES. Well . . . I think he's worried about his dad.

CATHY. His *dad*?

FRANCES. You know, the family thing. His having worked his way up, getting here. The family pride thing. You know, throw it all away.

RUTH. What do *you* think?

FRANCES. Well . . .

Pause.

COLIN. What *do* you think?

FRANCES (*turns*). Oh. Colin.

RUTH. Colin, Dave was after you.

COLIN. I'll bet he was.

CATHY *picks up the placards and manages a clenched-fist sign at* COLIN *as she goes out.*

CATHY. Good luck.

COLIN. Well, ta.

CATHY *takes her placards out right.* RUTH *decides to leave as well. She gets up, picks up the typewriter, and takes it out.* COLIN *and* FRANCES *left there.*

FRANCES. Well, then.

COLIN. Well.

Pause.

The solicitor informs me that I am about to put him in what he calls an impossible situation.

Being realistic, I suppose I ought to demand the impossible.

FRANCES. Them, having all the guns, but us the numbers.

COLIN. Well, exactly.

Slight pause.

I'm not sure, the technicalities. Whether I get arrested here and now. I brought my toothbrush, just in case.

Pause. COLIN *smiles.*

Well, here's looking at you, kid.

FRANCES *goes to* COLIN *and they embrace and kiss.* *Enter* DAVE.

DAVE. Ah, Colin – Oh.

DAVE *stands there. He scratches his ear. Finally,*

COLIN *turns to him.*

COLIN. Comrade.

DAVE *looks at his watch.*

COLIN (*with a shrug*). I self-criticse with all humility.

DAVE. So, are you proposing to harangue the throng?

COLIN. I thought I might try and catch the Chairman's eye.

DAVE. Then let the spectacular commence.

He gestures COLIN *out.* COLIN *kisses* FRANCES *again and follows.* DAVE *gives* FRANCES *a grin and a wink as he goes.* FRANCES *looks off right towards the meeting.* RUTH *enters behind her. She is smoking.*

RUTH. Friends, Romans, Comrades?

FRANCES. What? Oh, yes.

RUTH (*to herself*). So are they all, all honourable men.

But FRANCES *doesn't hear. The two* WOMEN *look offstage right at the meeting, which we hear:*

DAVE. Comrades. Can we start the meeting.

Hubbub.

Comrades. Can we have order.

Hubbub fading.

Thank you very much.

Hubbub fades

Right. Comrades, the meeting has been called, specifically, because of the University's action in taking out a court injunction against five comrades who they regard as being ringleaders of the occupation.

Buzz of reaction. Hisses. During this, CATHY *re-enters and nods at* RUTH *and* FRANCES *before leaning up against the table to smoke a cigarette and watch.*

Sadly, two of the five comrades concerned are unable to comply, or indeed not to comply with the order, as they graduated from the University last summer.

Laughter.

One of those who hasn't graduated however is Colin Cook,

secretary of Soc Soc. He's still very much around, in fact he's here, and I call on Comrade Cook to speak to the meeting.

Applause.
FRANCES *a smiling glance at* RUTH.

COLIN. Comrades, I have in my hand a piece of paper, issued in the High Court of Justice, which restrains me from entering or re-entering this building, and particularly from inciting or encouraging others to enter, re-enter or remain in the aforesaid building, upon pain of further legal action of a character unspecified.

A sound of ripping.

I now have in my hand two pieces of paper. And I'd like to incite and encourage you all to remain in this building.

Applause. It grows.
FRANCES *turns to* RUTH.

FRANCES. Magic. I mean, it's magic.

Mean, you read the history, the Paris Commune, Russian Revolution, mighty moments, everything is changed.

But for it to be happening now. To see it. Be it. And for me, to be with it, me, to be happening, too.

RUTH. Yes.

FRANCES *turns back to look at the meeting. Applause going on. Perhaps even people singing the Internationale.*

RUTH. Yes, it is indeed 1968. And everything's in question. Everything is challenged, everything is new. We don't demand, we occupy, because the plastic culture's melting on the stove of history.

Slight pause. FRANCES *has turned to her.*

So one does just wonder . . . Why the fuck we're still doing the typing and making the tea.

FRANCES *a little shrug.*

FRANCES. Now there you have me.

Blackout.

Scene Five.

Immediately, in the darkness, the Gloria from Bach's 'B Minor Mass'.

This scene takes place in ROSIE's *kitchen.* ROSIE *is at her worktop, between the hob and the fridge. On the worktop are a bottle of oil, a pepper grinder, a chopping block, a knife, bags of mushrooms and courgettes, a tin of baked beans and a tin opener.*

We are going to see a kind of culinary ballet in which ROSIE *prepares three meals. On three occasions during this, her husband* HOWARD *will enter with the phone on a long lead. He will wander back and forth with the phone, and go out again. He is wearing a business suit, though in his second entrance he has taken off his tie.*

He looks what he is, a highly motivated, upwardly mobile young junior manager.

It is January 1972.

ROSIE *puts two saucepans on the cooker. Then she takes a baby's bottle from the fridge, and puts it in one of the saucepans. Then she takes a third saucepan from the cupboard, opens the baked beans, and puts them in the saucepan and on the cooker.*

Enter HOWARD *with the phone.*

HOWARD. Uh huh. Uh huh. No, sure. No problem.

Yuh, mate, just off the plane. First port of call.

He winks at ROSIE.

Look, mate, I've just cleared them 20 grand. The least they can do is read a fucking memo.

He looks to ROSIE, *realising he's said 'fuck' in front of her. She smiles. He carries the phone out.*

So?

He's gone. ROSIE *takes two frying pans, puts oil in one and butter in the other, and puts both on the hob. She takes two steaks and a packet of fish fingers from the fridge.*

She puts the fish fingers in one of the frying pans.

She expertly chops the mushrooms.

Re-enter HOWARD.

HOWARD. No, no, I don't think that's a problem but we'd need to talk it through.

Hey, yuh. Why not. No hassle.

Well, I think we were going to a show or something, but it's nothing we can't shift.

He looks at ROSIE *and mouths 'Thursday'. She nods.*

Yuh. Sure. It's eminently changeable.

He goes.
ROSIE *grinds pepper on the steaks and pops them in the other frying pan with the mushrooms. She takes the baked beans off the cooker, stirs them, puts them back. She chops the courgettes.*
Slight panic – she's forgotten the fish fingers.
She takes their frying pan off the cooker and turns them over.
She finishes the courgettes and puts them in the third saucepan.
She goes out, re-enters with a bottle of wine and a corkscrew. She is opening the bottle as HOWARD *appears with a Lufthansa bag. As he speaks, he takes out a bottle and a jewelry case and puts them on the worktop in front of* ROSIE.

HOWARD. No, mate, I told you. Just back from Heathrow.

Yuh, well, I tell you, Frankfurt's better than Cologne.

Yuh, apparently the lights were out here too. All afternoon.

Right on, mate. What a bloody country.

He blows a kiss at ROSIE *and goes out.* ROSIE *puts down the bottle, opens the jewelry case, takes out a necklace and smiles.*

The Bach swells.

Scene Six

A baroque trumpet fanfare in the darkness. Not very well played. After the fanfare we hear a song and a fragment of an agit-prop play by RUTH, ANNE *and* TONY *(who played the trumpet). During it, the lights come up on a bare room in a squatted house. It is the spring of 1972. The play is being rehearsed in the next-door room. In this room,* SANDRA, *a nineteen-year-old working-class woman, is feeding her baby with a bottle. She is sitting on the floor, next to a primus on which is a saucepan of water.*
   A placard leans up somewhere. It reads 'Fuck the Family'. The play goes as follows:

VOICES. Onward Christian housewives
         Marching to the sink
         Providing what our husbands
         Demand to eat and drink

We milk their sunshine breakfasts
Bake our humble pie
We are drowned in fairy liquid
Raped by what we buy
Onward Christian housewives
Marching to the store
The image of the Master
Going on before.

TONY (*full ecclesiastical works*). And so, wilt thou, man –

RUTH. That's me?

TONY. That's you, have this Woman for thy wedded wife –

A knock at the outside door.

–wilt thou beat her, exploit her and scorn her, in her sickness
and your wealth, and forsaking all others –

Knock knock.

– except of course for those bits of stuff, crumpet, skirt, arse and
cunt on the side –

SANDRA. Hey. DOOR.

TONY. – that are every man's due and right, for as long as you feel
inclined?

RUTH. I certainly will.

SANDRA. Hey, DOOR.

TONY. And wilt thou, woman –

Knock knock knock.

SANDRA. Hey someone. DOOR.

ANNE. All *right.*

SANDRA *feeds her baby.*
ANNE *crosses the stage.*
*She is dressed in a parody wedding gown, festooned with pots, pans,
chains and symbols of degradation. She goes through the set and out.
Offstage, we hear her answer the door:*

ANNE. Yes? What is it?

FRANCES. We wondered if Ruth is about.

ANNE. What d'you want her for.

FRANCES. Well, we're from a thing called the Fight the Rent Act Campaign. We're building for a meeting.

ANNE. Oh, I see.

ANNE, COLIN and FRANCES come into the room.

ANNE. Right. Hold on.

She goes out the other side.
SANDRA clocks FRANCES's and COLIN's look to each other.

SANDRA. They're practising a play.

COLIN. I see.

FRANCES. D'you squat here?

SANDRA. Yuh. That's right.

Pause.

You're going to have a meeting?

FRANCES. Yes. D'you want to come?

SANDRA. What's it about?

FRANCES. It's about the fight against the Tory Rent Act.

SANDRA. Ah. I don't pay rent.

FRANCES. Well, still . . .

Slight pause.

The reason people have to squat, is rents. Bad housing, speculators shoving up the prices, so that they can make a million out of empty office blocks like Centre Point. I mean, you have to squat because you've nowhere else to live.

SANDRA. Well, yuh, that's not exactly why I –

But she's interrupted by the entrance of TONY, a young man carrying a trumpet and dressed as an Abbess. He walks across the stage. As he goes:

TONY. Good afternoon.

And out.

COLIN. Oh, hi.

SANDRA (*standing with her baby*). That's Tony. He's a Mother Superior.

SANDRA smiles, and goes out with the baby as RUTH enters. She is dressed as a Victorian employer.

RUTH. Hallo, Fran.

FRANCES. Don't tell me, let me guess. The Ruling Class.

RUTH. Dead right in one.

Enter ANNE. *She sits on the floor to do something to her costume. Pause.*

COLIN. The reason, looked you up, was cos we got a meeting planned, to fight the HFA, and thought perhaps –

RUTH. The HFA?

COLIN. Housing Finance Act.

RUTH. Oh.

COLIN. And we wanted someone from the squatting movement. Speaking. And we hoped it might be you.

RUTH. Well, I . . .

COLIN. We got a leaflet. It explains what's going on.

He hands RUTH *a leaflet.*
She reads it.
TONY *comes in, without the trumpet. He leans against a wall, waiting.*

FRANCES (*to* ANNE). What's the play for?

ANNE. Oh, it's the Festival of Light. Cliff Richard's lighting up a bloody beacon in the park. We're an alternative attraction. Kind of, powers of darkness.

COLIN *and* FRANCES *smile.*

Bit scary, really.

Slight pause.

It's a marriage play. Tony's the Church and State, and I'm the little woman wedded unto Capital.

COLIN. Oh, so you're kind of, the working class as well?

ANNE. Um . . .

RUTH *gives the leaflet to* COLIN.

RUTH. Thank you.

To ANNE *and* TONY.

Right. We better move.

ANNE (*standing*). Right then.

RUTH. Tony, have you got your bloody horn?

COLIN. Uh . . .

TONY. In the car.

RUTH. OK.

COLIN. Um . . .

RUTH. Yes?

COLIN. About the meeting –

RUTH. Meeting? No. Not interested. Sorry.

COLIN. Why?

RUTH. Oh, I just don't think that it's of much concern to us.

COLIN. But of course it's of concern –

RUTH. Otherwise, you'd be discussing wife-battering, and instead of big guns from the N.U.M. and Parliament, you'd have a woman on the platform.

Pause. COLIN *thrown.*

FRANCES. That is why we're here. We obviously think that women should be mobilised. That's why we're here.

RUTH. They should be mobilised.

FRANCES. That's right.

RUTH. Them forming, half the working class.

COLIN. Of course.

RUTH. The bottom half.

COLIN. Indeed.

RUTH. You having, as it were, the big guns, us the numbers. So. A token pussy on the platform. Add a little feminist appeal. Attract the cannon fodder.

COLIN. No, that's not –

RUTH. Met Sandra? She's got housing problems. Notably, the owner of her house keeps laying into her.

FRANCES. The landlord beats her up?

RUTH. Her husband.

Slight pause.

COLIN. Well, you could always bring – that up –

RUTH. Look, Colin, are you just naturally stupid or are you being deliberately obtuse?

COLIN. You tell me.

RUTH. Oh, I really don't think I can be bothered.

Pause.

FRANCES. This meeting's about housing. It's about taking on this Tory Government. It's about continuing, what started with the miners and the fight against the Industrial Relations Bill.
And I personally don't think it's possible, to emancipate our sex without emancipating the working class. I don't think you can just change your lifestyle and the rest follows. I don't think you can change the insides of people's heads without changing what's outside them first.

COLIN *decides not to say anything.*

ANNE. Hey, Ruth, does she mean we're going to have to wait until after the revolution?

RUTH. I think that's right, Anne. After which, of course, the family and all its works just melt away.

ANNE. You mean, like Engels thought, when women went to work, and had a boss, that male supremacy would just, kind of, collapse?

RUTH. That's right, whereas in fact, of course, what's happened is that working women have two jobs, one paid and one unpaid –

COLIN. Well, I think that's oversimp-

TONY. You know, what really gets right up my nose about Fred Engels?

Pause.

COLIN. No?

TONY. It's that his view of my lifestyle was summed up in the phrase 'degrading and perverted'. And what really does extend my nostrils about blokes like you, is when you say my way of living's alienating to the working class, it doesn't strike you that the working class is fucking alienating to me.

Pause.

COLIN. What did I say? When did I say that?

RUTH. Hey. I've got a wonderful idea. Why not let Tony address the meeting. Or Anne. Or Sandra. Or all of us. We'll all of us go 'long and speak. Or sing. Much better. Do a little turn. We'll really turn them on. Or p'raps they might be worried that we'll really turn them off?

COLIN. Do you want to talk about it seriously?

RUTH. No, not a lot. I'm bored. I really haven't got the energy, you know, to talk to you. In fact, I think I want to go.

Slight pause.

ANNE. Yuh, sure. Let's go.

She goes out. RUTH *picking up the placard.*

TONY. Right then.

TONY *goes out.*

FRANCES. Good luck.

RUTH. The same to you.

She goes out. Pause.

FRANCES. Well.

Pause. COLIN's *not going to say anything.*
FRANCES *feels she ought to say something.*

I mean, I'm not opposed to the demands, I mean of course there should be equal pay and free abortion. I just do find it difficult, to take that seriously a group of people arguing that the Queen's exploited by her footmen and her stable boys.

You know?

COLIN *a smile and a wink.*

COLIN. Well, here's looking at you, kid.

They are about to go when SANDRA *enters with another bottle. She kneels by the primus, to put it on to boil. She realises something. She looks up to* COLIN *and* FRANCES.

SANDRA. Hey, you got a match?

Blackout.

Scene Seven

In the darkness, 'Stand By Your Man' by Tammy Wynette.

After the change, fade under a burst of laughter and lights fade up on the scene. It is a small meeting of WOMEN, *in May 1975. They sit in a kind of circle. It is important that the focus of this scene is in the centre of it, directed from the* WOMEN *to each other, not at all out front, and even slightly excluding the audience.*

The WOMEN *are* RUTH, SANDRA, ROSIE *(who has her back to us) and* CATHY *who is now a college lecturer. She wears an abortion campaign badge.* RUTH *wears a Women's Movement badge.* ROSIE *and* RUTH *are smoking. The* WOMEN *are laughing. The laughter subsides, but whatever's just been said sparks one or two to revive the laughter, and the humour still bubbles through the first few lines.*

CATHY. You know, I really think we ought to talk about doing something.

SANDRA. Oh, ar. Voice of reason.

CATHY. I thought, perhaps what we were saying, nurseries . . .

ROSIE. I'm sorry, what was that?

RUTH. Last week, we talked about the lack of nursery facilities. We thought of doing something.

ROSIE. Doing what?

CATHY. Well, I did have some thoughts, in fact.

She finds a piece of paper.

SANDRA. Course, they might not need a nursery.

CATHY. I thought we might consider a three-pronged approach. First, we could raise a petition, for a nursery.

RUTH. Whereas, they might want something else.

I mean, this is quite a well-off area. A lot of women don't go out to work. They sit at home. Don't meet. Don't use the launderette.

They sit at home, just going quietly bonkers.

Perhaps they just need a place to meet. Perhaps we should think about a place for women to meet.

Pause.

CATHY. Well, I'm not sure where that would get us. I mean, I know a lot of women who'd love not to have to work. I feel there's things that are much more politically important.

RUTH. It's not politically important, then, that women sit at home going bonkers?

CATHY. No, that's not –

RUTH. In fact, I know, this woman. What you'd say, I s'pose you'd call, an unimportant, bored . . . And she has, I mean, this woman's made so bonkers by the role that unimportant way of life has forced her into, that she spends her day, her whole day, mind, just cooking, separate meals, for all her family. The baby's mush. The five-year-old's fish fingers. The eleven-year-old subsists on hamburgers, she's into haute cuisine and hubby's just gone vegan.

And that, of course, is leaving out the bloody dog.

And I do, frankly, feel –

ROSIE *jumps up. She's dropped her cigarette into the folds of her dress.*

ROSIE. Oh, God –

SANDRA. What's the matter?

ROSIE. Lost a fag. Oh, here . . .

She finds it. Sits again.

Ruin more frocks that way.

Pause. The incident has changed the atmosphere.

RUTH. I think, I mean, I think we're still not starting from ourselves. I think we're still frightened of confronting *our* wants, *our* fears, *our* rage, the way that we're oppressed by men, emotionally, intellectually, physically, day by day.

SANDRA. Oh, speak for yourself.

RUTH. What do you mean?

SANDRA (*parody*). 'What do you mean?'

Slight pause.

I just get a bit fed up when you talk as if the things you think and feel are what all women think and feel.

And I think in fact, sometimes, getting heavy and aggressive's just as – well –

ROSIE. I'd like –

They turn to her.

I'd like to know.

Slight pause.

Bit more about the woman cooks five meals a day.

Pause.

RUTH. You mean, 'bout who she –

ROSIE. Why she does it. How a person could.

Pause.

RUTH. Well. S'pose.

Slight pause.

She hasn't got a life. Life on her own. She's stored it, packaged it out, between her husband and her children. And she does it well. Her life is comfortable. Painless. Tranquil. Numb.

Pause.

Oh, it isn't easy. I don't find it easy. In the pub, a good time being had by all, and some bloke calls someone a cunt, or cracks a sexist joke, or peers at some girl's bottom. And it ain't easy, take him up on it, be heavy and aggressive, lay your scene on him, and he says, oh beg pardon but for Christ's sake I don't *mean* . . . And you've fucked up the good time. Ruined it. That really don't come easy.

SANDRA. No. No, I can see that.

Everyone except RUTH *picks up the joke. Then* RUTH *picks up the joke. The tension eases.*

RUTH. Liberated? I don't feel liberated. I feel like I just jumped off a cliff without a parachute.

CATHY. That's Germaine Greer.

Pause.

SANDRA. Right on.

Pause.

CATHY. But don't you think . . . don't you really think we should decide . . .

Pause. SANDRA *suddenly finds this the funniest thing in the world. It's completely infectious. All the women collapse laughing.*

Blackout.

Scene Eight

In the darkness, 'Black Jack Davy', from the LP, 'All Around My Hat', by Steeleye Span.
The lights on FRANCES's *flat.*
It is later the same night.
COLIN *is listening to the record which is on the record-player.*
He drinks a glass of wine and is reading a copy of International Socialism. In front of him, on the floor, is a two-litre bottle of red wine, another glass, and a tray with coffee things.
A full ashtray also on the floor.
COLIN's *coat over the back of the sofa.*
FRANCES *comes in, and* COLIN *takes off the record.*

FRANCES. She's putting the kids to bed.

COLIN. Where's she putting them?

FRANCES. Oh, one's in the study and the little girl'll sleep with Rosie in the spare room.

COLIN. Anything to help?

FRANCES. Don't think so.

FRANCES sits on the sofa and fills her glass.

Well, what a thing.

COLIN. So, what happened?

FRANCES. Well. Apparently she'd been to a women's meeting, some consciousness raising thing, and got home late, and he was furious, and made a crack about bra-burning and capow. She walked out. There and then. The kids and all.

COLIN. That is amazing.

FRANCES. I haven't seen her for years. Not properly, since she was married.

Pause.

Just like that. I think it's bloody marvellous.

Enter ROSIE.

Hi. Have you got them settled down all right?

ROSIE *crosses her fingers and sits. She's tired.*

Rosie, you met across a crowded pile of suitcases and children, but this is Colin.

ROSIE. Yes. Hallo.

COLIN. It's nice to meet you.

FRANCES. Colin was round. For dinner.

Pause.

COLIN. Speaking of which, I'll . . . go and do the kitchen.

FRANCES. Right.

COLIN *stands and goes out. During the following, we hear him whistle as he washes up.*

D'you want a glass of wine? Or coffee? Or, indeed, I think, somewhere some scotch?

ROSIE. No thank you. Later, p'raps.

FRANCES. OK.

Pause.

ROSIE. I have just left my fucking husband.

Long pause.

FRANCES. D'you want to talk about it?

ROSIE. Sorry?

FRANCES. Oh, that sounds as if you've just had a bereavement. I meant –

ROSIE. No. Not a bereavement. The reverse.

FRANCES. That's right.

Pause.

How did he take it?

ROSIE. Howard?

FRANCES. Yuh.

Pause.

ROSIE. Looked lost. Last thing of him I saw, just standing in the kitchen, looking at the rows of gleaming things. I really don't think, that he knew, what they were for.

I've got this odd contraption, dices onions. He just stood there, gazing at it, trying to work it out.

Enter COLIN *in what is obviously* FRANCES's *pinny. He has plastic gloves on. He is whistling. He puts down a clean ashtray, puts the dirty one on the tray and takes it out.*

FRANCES. He wasn't angry, then? Just lost?

ROSIE. Oh, he was wild with rage. Was like, you know, you lost things, lose a purse, a chequebook, and you're in a hurry, and you can't believe it's gone. You stand there, trying to think. You get a kind of, furious inertia.

He was standing, staring at my autochop, like that.

Pause.

FRANCES. Colin and I were saying, it's quite marvellous. To do it, just like –

ROSIE. No, not marvellous. Don't think. Not marvellous.

Pause.

I feel as if I've been asleep. A soft-down slumber. All these years. Faint voices, in the distance, through the doze. Half-heard. The world outside.

And then to wake up, find yourself, the middle of a nightmare, carnage all around, bits of your body ripped up on the bed . . . You want to shut your eyes again, turn over, pull the blankets tight.

You can't. But it's not, marvellous.

FRANCES *smiles.*

FRANCES. No. Sure.

A warm pause. Enter COLIN, *without the pinny and gloves. He sits, lights a cigarette.*

COLIN (*to* ROSIE). Do you want some wine?

ROSIE. No thanks.

COLIN *gestures to* FRANCES *with the bottle.* FRANCES *nods, so* COLIN *pours them both wine.*

What do you do?

COLIN. Well, for a living, I'm a teacher. But my main thing's postgraduate research.

ROSIE. What into?

COLIN. The British Labour Movement during World War Two.

ROSIE. I see.

Pause.

FRANCES. I don't know if you saw, there was a series, on Granada, last year, 'bout wartime Liverpool. Colin did a lot of the research.

ROSIE. I didn't see it, no. Sounds wonderful.

Pause.

COLIN. What was this meeting that you went to?

ROSIE. Oh, it was a group of women. Met one of them through Damion's school. Asked me to come along.

COLIN. What was it about?

ROSIE. Well, it wasn't, really, quite *about* anything. I mean, it was about day nurseries, but not *about*.

Slight pause.

I'm sorry . . .

FRANCES. Know what you mean.

COLIN. I used to be very suspicious of all that.

ROSIE. All what?

COLIN. Oh, small group politics. In fact, the Women's Movement. Fran will tell you.

FRANCES. Fran will tell you.

COLIN. Yes. I mean, I used to think it was, just therapy. Trying to find individual solutions to problems that were essentially collective.

FRANCES *grins at* ROSIE.

I think, in fact, it was a kind of reaction, to the sixties, you know, all that free your head stuff, and we all reacted very strongly, in the opposite direction, kind of bend the stick, particularly with the Tory Government, the revival of industrial militancy, and so on.

COLIN *is warming to his theme.*

ROSIE *is looking at* COLIN, *trying to concentrate, a fixed and nervous smile on her face.*

But I think that was a great mistake, or anyway, mistake to *keep* that kind of prejudice. Because the kind of politics the Women's Movement's into, small group, consciousness, particularly, I think, the concern with raising consciousness, can make a major contribution to the wider struggle, as a whole, and –

ROSIE. Excuse me, would you shut up please?

Pause.

COLIN. Beg pardon?

ROSIE. Would you, please, mind shutting up?

Slight pause. She's nearly crying.

I'm sorry . . .

COLIN (*looks to* FRAN). Uh . . .

FRANCES. Colin, Rosie has just . . .

COLIN (*to* ROSIE). Look, I'm –

The phone rings.

FRANCES. Shit.

She looks at her watch.

Oh, who the fuck.

She stands and goes out to the phone. COLIN *and* ROSIE *don't know what to say, so they listen to the conversation.*

FRANCES (*off*). Hallo, Frances Lockett.

Oh, Steve.

Yes, they said at the branch they hadn't arrived.

Well, of course it's urgent. It's also your fault.

Look –

Look, Steve . . .

Look, Steve, can I get this straight . . . That's right, can I get it straight that you are seriously . . .

You're seriously ringing me at two a.m. to ask me to get up at six, drive thirteen miles and meet a fucking train?

I mean, you are of course joking. I mean, you are pulling my leg.

Oh, fuck off, Steve.

That's right.

Slam of phone. FRANCES *re-enters.*

COLIN. Who was it?

FRANCES. Oh, some creep from rank and file. He wanted me to get up in four hours and go and get some leaflets off Red Star.

COLIN. Now, look, I hope you told him –

FRANCES. Yes, of course I told him.

Pause.

Blokes. The bloody nerve.

Pause.
COLIN *glances at his watch.*
FRANCES *seizes the time.*

Uh, Col, I know it's late, but you wouldn't mind not staying, would you?

COLIN. Sorry?

FRANCES. See, I think it might be . . . Mean, I'd put you up, but Rosie's kids and all.

COLIN. You'd Put Me Up?

FRANCES. I think it would be simpler if you went.

Pause.
COLIN *stands.*

COLIN. Fran, could I have a word? outside?

Pause.

FRANCES. Oh, all right. If you want to.

They go out.
ROSIE *left there. She picks up the International Socialism, but is really listening – as are we – to the conversation from off.*

COLIN. So what's all this about?

FRANCES. Well, I'd just rather if you didn't stay.

COLIN. Why not?

FRANCES. Well, just, it's difficult.

COLIN. What's difficult about it?

FRANCES. Well, you –

COLIN. And I would point out that usually when I stay the spare room doesn't come into it.

FRANCES. That's not the point.

COLIN. What is the point?

FRANCES. It's just . . . I want to talk to Rosie.

COLIN. Well, who's stopping you?

FRANCES. Oh, *Colin*.

COLIN. Have I said something wrong? Look, of course I'm sorry if I . . . Look, I did get out of your way. That's why I did the washing up.

FRANCES. Well, thanks a lot.

COLIN. Oh, for heaven's –

FRANCES. Colin, go away.

Pause.

I'm sorry. But please go away.

Pause.

COLIN. I'll get my coat.

He comes into the room. He decides not to ask ROSIE *for his magazine back.* ROSIE *realises she's sitting on his coat. She gets up.* COLIN *is trying very hard not to show his anger.*

COLIN. Nice to meet you, Rosie.

ROSIE. Yes. And you.

He meets FRANCES *coming in.*

FRANCES. Night-night.

COLIN *goes.*
ROSIE *pours herself a glass of wine.*
FRANCES *sits.*

ROSIE. I'm sorry, if I . . .

FRANCES. No.

Pause.

ROSIE. I thought, to start with, that he lived here.

FRANCES. Nope. We stopped all that two years ago.

Now, we have this, well arrangement. You know, dinner and a fuck from time to time. Just as and when the inclination grabs us.

Sadly, like all informal, non-coercive, liberated and relaxed arrangements, it's extremely difficult to de-arrange.

ROSIE. I see.

FRANCES. It's tricky, cos he's given me so much. Well, in a way, he gave me everything.

Pause.

Look. An example. At the NUT, the teachers' conference, a year or two ago. And I proposed this motion. And I had to force them, put it on the agenda. And I did. And won it.

Quite a triumph. You know, points of order, citing precedent, procedure, challenging the chair. A mighty victory. But I came off shaking. Really shaking. Blubbering. Quite awful. And, well, Col was there, and did his stuff, and rallied round, and pulled me back together. Generously giving. As he always is. And does. But, still . . . (*Pause.*) I'm sorry, it's not –

ROSIE. Go on.

FRANCES. It's just . . . That Col is Peter Pan. He doesn't alter. Oh, the words, the ideas even, change. I mean you heard him, and I may say on his attitude to feminism in the early days, the half he did not tell you, but he . . . Underneath it all, he's still the little boy who got arrested at the sit-in and was marched off, all white-faced and brave, to jail.

ROSIE. He went inside?

FRANCES. One night. Then he got fined a hundred and we raised it and they let him go.

Not that it wasn't, in its way, quite brave . . .

But always, on his terms. And never, if it threatens anything, inside.

And what is even worse, is that I look at him, his busy-ness, routine, unchanging and unbending energy, the lack of any kind of pain or challenge, and I see myself.

See Me.

Pause.
ROSIE *laughs.*

Not inquisitorially:

So what's funny?

ROSIE. Well. Must tell you. Speaking of, changes.

She leans forward to FRANCES. *For the first time, she's relaxed.*

Was the other day. Was playing pantomimes with Sophie. It's a game, to guess the end. And I was doing Sleeping Beauty. And I had done the bit about the curse, and how the princess fell asleep, and years and years passed by and then I asked her, do you know what happened next.

And then she looks at me – you know the way they do, that effortless superiority – and says, oh yes, mum, know *that* one. This prince turns up, he finds the princess, kisses her, she wakes up and he turns into a frog.

FRANCES *laughs.*

My darling, let me press your cheery lips to –

ROSIE *turns into a frog.*

Rivet rivet rivet.

FRANCES *laughs.*
The two women frog away at each other.

FRANCES. Rivet rivet rivet.

ROSIE. Rivet rivet.

FRANCES. Oh that they all would.

ROSIE. What?

FRANCES. Turn into frogs.

They laugh.

Now look, comrade person, for the sake of the international proletarian struggle, you've just got to go and – rivet rivet rivet.

ROSIE. Hello Rosie How's Yerself You Burnt Yer Bra Yet How

About A Bit Of Liberation Huh Know What I –rivet rivet rivet.

FRANCES. Yes of *course* I'll do the dishes darling but I'll do them when *I* – rivet rivet rivet rivet.

ROSIE. Oh now come on petal come on tulip after all it's Saturday oh come on flower why not – rivet rivet.

FRANCES. Oh come on sweetheart, mean, all very well, but after all it's hardly real politics, now is it?

Pause. That's slightly too close to the bone for a second. But then:

Rivet. Rivet. Rivet.

The laughter again. And this time the frog imitation gets out of hand, and mutates into a kind of game, with much thrashing of arms, which provokes a memory of a similar game long past and the following lines:

FRANCES. Hey – hey – I must –

ROSIE. You must –

FRANCES. – improve . . .

The laughter finally dies.

The time. I teach at nine.

ROSIE. Please miss you know your stocking's got a great big – rivet rivet rivet.

This sets them off again.
Eventually, the laughter dies.

Look. Is it Ok if I stay.

FRANCES. Oh, yes, of course. You must.

ROSIE. I mean, I'll pay you rent.

FRANCES. Now, come on, what d'you use for money?

ROSIE. Ah.

Slight pause.

For money. Use.

She taps the side of her nose in a conspiratorial fashion. She goes out and returns with a cardboard box. She sits and take out a necklace.

Gifts.

She drops the necklace. Picking out another couple of trinkets:

Gifts from my man to me.

She drops the trinkets. Finding more:

Hundreds of glittering gifts. Gifts of his love. Generously given.

She drops more trinkets, picks out more.

Given so much. Given me everything.

She upends the box on the floor.

I'm going into trade.

Blackout.
'It's In His Kiss', by Linda Lewis, covers the change.

Scene Nine

The music fades as lights come up on a school cloakroom.
    It is the next day.
    The cloakroom is represented by a bench, about six feet long, underneath which are two vertically divided shelves for shoes. Above the bench is a row of pegs on which overcoats, hats, lacrosse and hockey sticks, etc. hang.
    There are two SCHOOLGIRLS *on the bench.*
    One is TRISHA, *who sits, facing out front, adjusting her make-up in a small mirror.*
    DENISE *lies on her tummy, her head cupped in her hands, smoking.*
    A magazine lies on the bench in front of her, though it is not immediately clear, when she speaks, that she is quoting from it.
    A few moments, then:

DENISE. Hey, Trisha.

TRISHA. Yuh?

DENISE. It's happened.

TRISHA. Yuh?

DENISE. You've met the Boy Of Your Dreams.

    Pause.

TRISHA. Oh. Right.

DENISE. Are you first attracted to him . . .

TRISHA. Yuh?

DENISE. By his brooding good looks and exotic air of mystery?

TRISHA. Um . . .

DENISE. Or his sentimental, old-world habits, buying flowers, always opening the door for you?

TRISHA. Tt, well . . .

DENISE. His line in witty and sophisticated chat –

TRISHA. Oh, I dunno . . .

DENISE. Or p'raps his friendly cheerful manner turned-up nose and happy smile?

Pause.

TRISHA. Don't think his turned-up nose.

DENISE (*finding a pencil to mark the score in*). No way his turned-up nose.

TRISHA. I s'pose, on balance, brooding good looks and exotic air of mystery.

DENISE. OK.

She pencils it in.

I think I'm going for the witty chat.

TRISHA. Oh, yuh. What's next?

DENISE. Ok you've caught your fella and the big night comes. Your date is –

TRISHA'*s noticed someone coming.*

TRISHA. Hey –

DENISE. What is it?

TRISHA. It's The Droop.

DENISE *looks off, quickly, stubs her cigarette out in one of the shoes in the shelves beneath her, turns and catches* TRISHA *who is trying to hide behind the coats, pulls her back.* DENISE *sits up, her feet on the bench.*

TRISHA, *checking with* DENISE, *sits too.* MR BREWER *comes in. He is a schoolmaster in his mid-thirties.*

BREWER. Ah. Here we are. Patricia and Denise. Playing hookey in the changing room. Again.

Pause.

DENISE's *tactic is to sit stock still, ignoring* BREWER.
TRISHA *follows this tactic, but with less assurance, and the occasional glance at* DENISE *to confirm what she's supposed to do.*

Yesterday morning it was geography we skipped. Somewhat to my surprise. Seeing as how Denise likes geography. Insofar as she finds anything of interest, geog is it. Strange people from strange lands. Some of them stranger, even, than herself.

Pause.

And yesteraft we missed our maths. On this occasion, was a little shaken by Patricia. Cos Patricia's good at mathematics. Even very good. Her little chums, Denise included, wouldn't recognise a logarithm if one slid up and bit them, but Patricia can square a root and map a matrix like there's no tomorrow. So, we must just hope and pray that she recalls how few of them she's got before she's thrown upon the tender mercies of the Joint Matriculation Board.

Pause.

And today, right now, in fact, it's metalwork. Fought long and hard for, metalwork. So we would not be stereotyped. Demeaned, by being forced into traditional roles.

Pause.

Why are we not in metalwork, dear pupils? Why, despite all the efforts of our struggling sisters, have we cut our class?

DENISE *turns very slowly and looks at* BREWER. *It is a stare of not inconsiderable contempt.* TRISHA, *after a glance, tries the same. Hold. Then:*

All right. I'll get your tutor. She will talk to you. Who knows, and work a miracle, and make the dumb to speak.

He walks out.
DENISE *puts her legs down, picks up the magazine and reads:*

DENISE (a) Boating on a lily-covered lake and listening to the nightingales. (b) Ten pin bowling at your local alley with his gang of madcap friends. (c) Quiet dinner in a wayside country inn with old oak beams above a roaring fire. (d) Rave-up at the trendy highclass London disco where you sip champagne and dance till dawn.

TRISHA. The lily-covered lake.

DENISE. The rave-up.

Pencils in.

Right.

TRISHA *stands, biting her lip, clearly worried by the* BREWER *incident.*

S'only Lockup.

TRISHA. Yuh.

She sits down again.

What happens next.

DENISE (*reading*). (3) Afterwards.

TRISHA. After what?

DENISE. The Date.

TRISHA. Oh. 'Course.

DENISE. He either walks you home beneath the blossom in your local churchyard. Or you ride on horseback home across the windswept moors beneath the brooding sky. Or, he buys you a chop suey at the Chinese take-away –

TRISHA. Yuck.

DENISE. Yuh, or else you speed along the freeway in his silver Lamborghini.

Pause. TRISHA *not sure. She takes the magazine, glances at it. She looks at the pop star pin-up on the opposite page.*

TRISHA. Hey. D'you think he looks a bit like Gary?

DENISE. Gary?

TRISHA. Yuh.

Pause.

DENISE. I think I fancy being driven in his silver whatsit.

TRISHA. Ooh, I think the ride across the windswept moor . . .

DENISE. You'll catch your death.

TRISHA. Safer than you are in his bloody Lamborghini.

Pause.

DENISE. Gary.

TRISHA (*slightly coy*). Yuh.

DENISE. What about Brian?

TRISHA. Oh, he's boring.

DENISE. Gary's boring.

TRISHA. Gary *isn't*.

DENISE. How do you know?

TRISHA. Can *tell*.

DENISE looks round.

DENISE. Here she comes.

She takes the magazine back and reads as FRANCES *comes in*:

Right, question four. Fantastic! Yesterday he said he was in love with you forever and he pledged you'd never part. You know it's true, cos he went on to say:

FRANCES. Hallo.

Pause.

TRISHA. 'Lo, Miss.

Slight pause. DENISE *a kind of wave.*

FRANCES. I was asked to have a word with you. By Mr Brewer.

TRISHA. Yes, Miss.

FRANCES. You're supposed to be in class. In metalwork.

Slight pause.

Can I ask why you're not there?

DENISE. Well –

Thinks better of it.

S'boring, miss.

FRANCES. I see.

Pause. TRISHA, *sensitively*:

TRISHA. Mean, s'no more boring than the other lessons, Miss. I mean, we think that needlework and cooking's a right pain as well.

FRANCES smiles. She sits on the bench.

DENISE *moves a little.*

FRANCES. What are you reading?

She picks up the magazine.

Which question are you on?

Pause. TRISHA *not sure whether to reply.* DENISE *slightly impatient:*

DENISE. The one 'bout what he says to you just after he's said he loves you and you'll never part.

FRANCES. I see.

She puts down the magazine. TRISHA *takes a decision, picks up the magazine, and reads, to* FRANCES:

TRISHA. His life's been just spent waiting for a girl like you. He lost his head to you in that first moment that you met but was too shy to say. He'd like it if this moment stayed forever and he'll never let you go. He loves you cos he needs you and his whole life's changed.

Pause.

Which would your fella say, Miss?

FRANCES (*caught out slightly*). Well, I don't know many men, who'd, well, be likely to say anything like that.

TRISHA/DENISE (*sympathetically*). Oh, Miss.

FRANCES. Not sure I'd want to.

TRISHA. Wouldn't you?

FRANCES. I mean, it's not my type of dream.

DENISE. What *is*, then, Miss?

Pause.

FRANCES. Well, I . . . I like a man who treats me as a human being, lets me be independent, and who knows how to wash his own socks.

TRISHA *and* DENISE *look at each other, deeply shocked.*

I mean, come on, you can't seriously think that any real person's going to talk like that?

Pause. The GIRLS *clam.*
Then DENISE, *quietly:*

DENISE. Think how they do talk, Miss.

FRANCES. What do you mean?

The GIRLS *don't reply.*
The bell goes.
It stops.

Well. There we are. I'm afraid it looks as if Mr Brewer has been denied the satisfaction of your unwilling presence in the metal –

TRISHA *and* DENISE *are giggling.*

What's so funny?

They giggle on.

Oh, come on, what's the joke?

TRISHA. Just, Mr Brewer, getting satisfaction, Miss.

FRANCES. Yes? So?

Pause.
TRISHA *glances at* DENISE.
DENISE, *with an 'in for a penny' shrug:*

DENISE. He's called the Droop Miss.

FRANCES. Droop?

DENISE. You know, like Brewer's . . .

FRANCES. Ah.

She laughs. The GIRLS *laugh as well.*
The three of them are having a high old time until FRANCES *notices*
MR BREWER *standing there. He wears a tracksuit.*

Ah. Mr Brewer.

She stands.
The GIRLS *are having trouble.*

Yes. Well, Mr Brewer, I've had a word, of course, Denise, Patricia, and it is – they say it definitely – won't occur again. No question. Of it. Happening. As you might say, again. It's all, um, sorted out, uh, Mr Brewer.

FRANCES *pushes her way past* BREWER. *Lights up on two chairs*
elsewhere on the stage – representing the staff room. BREWER *follows*
FRANCES *to the staff room as the lights on the changing room fade.*

Scene Ten

In the staffroom, FRANCES *takes out marking.* BREWER *takes off his tracksuit. He wears black refereeing kit.*

BREWER. I mean, don't get me wrong, Miss Lockett.

I mean, I'm quite delighted you're so keen their independent little personalities should be developed. Most impressed, technique of yours of treating them as if they're human beings.

He goes out left.
Shouts from off:

And I quite understand, of course, and sympathise, your problems in that project, with Denise. Her relationship with the human race being no more than mildly coincidental.

He re-enters with a pair of black socks and football boots. He sits on the other chair and changes his shoes and socks:

And while of course it's true the only way we could assist Denise vocationally would be help her polish up her lock-picking, there is the minor matter of the fact that she's encouraging Patricia, too, into a life of crime. And while of course it's true that dear Patricia's hardly set fair for an Exhibition to St Hilda's, she does have a little spark, a little talent, limited, 'tis true, but there.

He stands.

A talent which Denise, of course, is set on snuffing out.

He goes out right.
Shouts from off:

Now, I appreciate, of course, your view of things is somewhat different. For you, of course, they are not little girls at all, they're victims of oppression, they're exploited by the running dogs of bourgeois ideology.

He re-enters with a football, which he puts down by his chair:

And thus are nothing more or less than willing or unwilling soldiers of the Revolution. Soldierettes.

BREWER *picks up his normal shoes and socks, goes out left, continues shouting:*

And, consequently, what is best for them, is quite irrelevant. Or even harmful. As it might dilute their military zeal.

BREWER *re-enters, carrying a whistle, and putting a notebook in his top pocket.*

And, of course, their actual wishes, what they want, come even further down the list of your priorities.

BREWER *putting his shirt inside his shorts and his whistle round his neck.*

But, nonetheless, they are still little girls, their prospects and their visions grossly limited. Perhaps, for one of them, an 'O' or two, so she can climb, at least, the bottom rung . . . But I do quite appreciate, for you, that even that would be no more than just a sell-out to the patriarchial bourgeoisie.

FRANCES (*decides to react*). Uh, Mr Brewer –

BREWER. Miss Lockett, don't imagine for a moment, I don't understand your game.

He blows his whistle to test it, and makes to stride out.

FRANCES. But, Mr Brewer –

BREWER (*turns back*). Yes?

FRANCES. You've forgotten your ball, Mr Brewer. It would never do to go without your ball.

She picks up the ball and throws it to BREWER.
He smiles, rather more knowingly than we might expect.

BREWER. Thank you so much, Ms. Lockett.

He goes out. FRANCES *stands.*

Scene Eleven

Music fades. Lights on the changing room. TRISHA *has gone.* DENISE *sits on the bench. She's counting money on her lap. Her handbag beside her.*

FRANCES *joins her.*

FRANCES. 'Lo, Denise.

DENISE, *quickly puts her arms over the money.*

DENISE. 'Lo, Miss.

FRANCES. You're not at games?

DENISE. I got a mum's note, Miss.

FRANCES. Oh, yes, of course.

Pause.
FRANCES *sits beside* DENISE.
DENISE *doesn't quite know what to do about the money.*

FRANCES. Do I assume . . .

DENISE. What Miss?

FRANCES. That we have found the mastermind behind the fourth form poker ring?

Pause. DENISE *raises her arms.*

DENISE. Well . . . only 80p, Miss.

FRANCES. Only 80p.

DENISE *puts her money into her handbag. She realises* FRANCES *is not going to go away. So, to make conversation:*

DENISE. D'you play cards, Miss?

FRANCES. Not with you I don't.

Pause.

So what was the result of the quiz?

DENISE. Eh?

Slight pause.

Oh, yuh. Quiz. Well, um.

Slight pause.

Trisha was a one hundred per cent reality-proof romantic. She dreamt of faraway places and strange exotic experiences. She went for blokes who promised brooding mystery and just a hint of danger. Her fault was that perhaps her dreamy nature tended to like blind her to the faults of others.

FRANCES. Yes, I see. And you?

DENISE. I am not one for the simple romantic pleasures am I cos I want a life of luxury and glamour p'raps I set my sights too high. Sez they.

Pause.

F'y'ask me, it's a load of rubbish.

FRANCES. Well, there I might agree with you.

DENISE. Yuh. Well.

Pause.

Mean, Trish just buys 'em for the pinups and the beauty hints. Like me, prefer me thrillers.

FRANCES. Thrillers?

DENISE. Yuh.

FRANCES. What kind of thrillers do you like?

DENISE. Oh, you know. Ed McBain. And that.

Pause.

FRANCES. My favourite's Raymond Chandler. Have you read his books?

DENISE *looking neutral.*

The Big Sleep? Things like that?

Pause.

DENISE *decides to risk it.*

DENISE. 'I walked into the room. Neither of the people in the room took any notice of me, which was odd, cos only one of them was dead.'

FRANCE's *delighted smile makes* DENISE *think she's maybe gone too far.*

I haven't read 'em all. I mean, they're always taken out, the library.

FRANCES. You could, I mean, I've quite a selection.

Slight pause.

You could, perhaps, come round.

DENISE. Uh, well . . .

FRANCES. I don't suppose you ever babysit?

Pause.

DENISE. Uh, Miss, you got a . . .

FRANCES. No, not me. A friend staying with me.

DENISE. Oh.

Slight pause.

Yuh. Sure. Be nice.

Slight pause.

Could I bring Trish?

FRANCES. Of course. I'll have a word, my friend, and let you know, an evening.

DENISE. Fine.

Pause.

FRANCES. You like Trish, don't you?

DENISE. Yuh. Best friend.

Pause.

FRANCES. Denise, what did you mean, you said, this morning, bout the way that boys talk. What d'you mean by that?

DENISE. Eh?

She remembers.

Oh. Oh, yuh.

Pause.

Well, just. Like, humping. Having. It, an'. Getting it. And slit. An' up your hole. And shouting, come on, show's your hangers. Shouting out, she got her rags on. Scrubbers. Slags.

Slight pause.

An all.

FRANCES. You needn't take all that.

DENISE. I don't.

FRANCES. But some girls do.

Pause.

DENISE. I don't.

FRANCES. You shouldn't.

Pause.
DENISE *looks at* FRANCES, *suspiciously.*

DENISE. Eh, Miss. You women's lib?

FRANCES. Yes. If you like.

Pause.

Because I think you shouldn't take all that. Because I think that that's a waste of you. I think you've got a better life, a life of your own.

Pause.
DENISE *says nothing.*
FRANCES *glances at her watch and stands.*

Well, p'raps I ought to go. I'll let you know about the babysitting?

DENISE. Yuh. F'you like.

FRANCES. Well, cheerio, Denise.

DENISE. Yuh. Cheers.

FRANCES goes out.
DENISE *sits there.*
Then enter TRISHA *in hockey gear. She's dripping wet.*
She goes to her peg, finds her mirror in a coat pocket, and a brush and comb, sits, looks at herself.

TRISHA. It's raining. Bloody raining.

She looks at her hair.

Mean, just look. Me split ends got split ends.

She tries to brush her hair.

Met *Gary* in the corridor. Me hair, like *this*.

DENISE. Oh, *Gary*.

TRISHA *turns to* DENISE, *smiling, as if it's a joke between them.*

Oh, bloody *Gary*.

DENISE *looks away from* TRISHA, *who stops smiling.*
TRISHA *decides to shrug it off.*

TRISHA. Eh, that the Lockup, talking to you.

DENISE (*assenting*). Mm.

TRISHA. So what she want to talk about?

Slight pause.

DENISE. She wanted us to babysit.

TRISHA. She got a baby?

DENISE. No she got a friend.

Pause.

TRISHA. I like the Lockup. Mean, she's really smart. Them Lotus shoes.

DENISE. You what?

TRISHA. Her shoes. What else she say?

DENISE. She talked, she said I shouldn't waste myself.

TRISHA. You shouldn't what?

DENISE. She said, like I'd got a better life.

TRISHA. What, better than –

DENISE. Life of me own.

TRISHA. Eh, Den.

DENISE *looks at her.*

Eh, Den. D'you think I'm 'shallow'?

DENISE. No. Who says?

TRISHA. Oh, just . . . A Lack Of Character?

DENISE. You what?

TRISHA. The Droop said once. I'm shallow. Need, like to develop character.

DENISE. Once asked me mum, if I was pretty. And she said, don't worry 'bout it pet, cos you got character. Mean, like I think she meant, instead.

Pause.

TRISHA. I think you're pretty.

DENISE *shrugs.*

You're me best friend, Den. I hope we'll always be the way we are. I hope we'll never change.

D'you promise, that we'll always be?

Pause.

DENISE. Oh, yuh. I promise.

TRISHA. Really?

DENISE. Sure.

Pause.

Do you? D'you promise, really?

TRISHA. Yuh, I promise.

Slight pause.

Cross my heart and hope to die.

Pause. TRISHA *looks at herself in the mirror.*

Oh, just look me bloody hair.

TRISHA *and* DENISE *hold. Lights change.* DEBBIE *and* SHARON *enter. They are 15-year-old ravers.* DEBBIE *is near* TRISHA *and* SHARON *near* DENISE.

DEBBIE. She'd always been the dreamy one, forever longing for the one true love that would transport her into endless bliss.

SHARON. She'd always been the do-or-die type, full of madcap notions, wild ideas and harebrained schemes.

FRANCES *appears.*

FRANCES. But still, they were the very best of friends, and it seemed impossible that anything or anyone could come between them.

Start the music.

DEBBIE. And so little did she think –

SHARON. And who'd have thought –

FRANCES. And how could – how could she have known . . .

Swell music: Linda Lewis, Old School Yard.
Lights fade.
Interval.

Scene Twelve

The flashing lights of the Youth Club disco. Play Suzi Quatro: 'You Can't Make Me Love You' from the LP Your Momma Won't Like Me. *The words of the song fit round the lines in the scene. Enter* DEBBIE *and* SHARON, *looking extraordinary.*

SUZI QUATRO. Well you thought you got an angel
But I tell you, it just ain't so

DEBBIE. It was disco-night at the Youth Club, and all the crowd were there.

SUZI QUATRO. This cherub-looking momma
Ain't no baby, doncha know

SHARON. Sharon and Debbie and all the other girls dolled up to the nines.

SUZI QUATRO. When you touch me you set me aglow

DEBBIE. There was only one thing missing –

SUZI QUATRO. And when I'm in your arms, I really don't wanna go
. . .

SHARON. So where are the fellas, huh?

SHARON and DEBBIE *dance to the chorus, during which,* GARY *makes his entrance. He is about 16, chews gum, and leers a lot. He stands there, leering.*

SUZI QUATRO. Well you can make me want you
But I ain't gonna love you
Aint gonna be the one at home
Waiting for you
I feel the rhythm but I never gonna feel the pain

SHARON and DEBBIE *stop dancing. They turn and see* GARY *and freeze:*

SHARON/DEBBIE. Wow – It's – GARY.

GARY *leans somewhere.*

SUZI QUATRO. Lady little lady
I'm an actress in your game

DEBBIE. And it had happened, there he was, standing silhouetted in the flashing lights . . .

SUZI QUATRO. Dancing and romancing
What you trying to gain

SHARON. Gary the fifth-form heart-throb, the scrummiest guy in the school . . .

SUZI QUATRO. Just lead me to your bed

DEBBIE. And there was only one question:

SUZI QUATRO. But if I stay all night
I'm gonna get inside your head

SHARON. Which of us was to be the lucky girl tonight?

SHARON and DEBBIE, *once again dance through the Chorus.* GARY *leans, leers and looks horrible. And, at the end,* DENISE *enters, looking amazing.*

SUZI QUATRO. Well, you can make me want you
　　But I ain't gonna love you
　　Ain't gonna be the one at home
　　Waiting for you
　　I feel the rhythm but I never gonna feel the pain

Same routine for SHARON *and* DEBBIE, *though this time, they look to* DENISE.

DENISE. Well hi there gang.

During the middle-eight instrumental, SHARON, DEBBIE *and* DENISE *go into a conversational huddle as a spot fades up on* TRISHA *at the side of the stage. She is dressed in a dressing gown, and wears a headscarf.*

TRISHA. It was dance night at the Youth Club. But for once I had chosen to stay at home and cram my math. I knew that my friend Denise was going to the hop, but I never dreamt that very night that she would take my world and dash it into little pieces.

She stays there.
The three GIRLS *break huddle.*

DENISE. S'Ok, you wanna try me?

DENISE *marches over to* GARY *as:*

SUZI QUATRO. Just like the rain is falling
　　Tears fall from my eyes

DENISE. Hey you.

GARY. Who me?

DENISE. Yuh you.

SUZI QUATRO. You know, the way you feel, for me
　　Came as no surprise

DENISE. You wanna dance?

GARY. I wanna what?

DENISE. You heard.

SUZI QUATRO. I guess I'll be moving on

DENISE. Well, d'ya wanna or doncha?

SUZI QUATRO. Cos another lover's are
　　Waiting for me to come

GARY. Well – I s'pose – yuh, l'right.

DENISE *takes* GARY *to the floor and they go into an uncomfortable clinch and freeze, as*:

SUZI QUATRO. Well, you can make me want you
But I ain't gonna be the one at home
Waiting for you
I feel the rhythm but I'm never gonna feel the pain

TRISHA. Oh, Denise, Denise, how could you –

SUZI QUATRO. I feel the rhythm but I never gonna feel the pain

Backed by the staccato chords that end the song, DENISE *suddenly pulls back from* GARY.
Her face is screwed up.
She wipes her mouth with her hand.
She looks at her hand.
She looks, in some disgust, at the boy GARY.
Blackout as the song ends, and at once:

DISC JOCKEY. And OK all you luscious lasses out there, it's turning up the tranny time, yes, yes, it's Les'n'Eric and the lovely boys, the b-b-b-Bay City Rollers with b-b-b-bye bye baby . . .

Play the Bay City Rollers: 'Bye Bye Baby'.

Scene Thirteen

Lights on TRISHA'S *room. The record goes on.*
   TRISHA *sits, in a slip, pinning up a dress, on a cushion on the floor. Beside her is a Snoopy mug containing, as it happens, Pernod, and the opened-parcel which contained the dress. Also the tranny from which the Rollers are proceeding.*
   DENISE *lies on the bed, smoking, reading a magazine, and also drinking Pernod from a Snoopy mug. The actual bottle is near her.*
   TRISHA *switches off the radio, raises her glass.*

TRISHA. So then. The Joint Matriculation Board.

DENISE. Its tender mercies.

TRISHA. An' all that.

They drink. TRISHA *looks in her glass.*

TRISHA. What's this again?

   DENISE *waves the bottle at* TRISHA.

   Pernod.

DENISE. It's oh.

TRISHA. Y'what?

DENISE. Pernod.

TRISHA. I see. It's nice.

Pause.

So where you get it?

DENISE. Waitrose Winemart. Slipped it under me potatoes.

TRISHA. *Den.* One day you'll get picked up, you know.

DENISE. Well I should be so lucky.

Pause.
TRISHA's *finished pinning.*
She stands:

TRISHA. Right then. Moment, all been waiting for.

DENISE *rolls over and watches* TRISHA *as she puts on the frock.*

Well, then. What you think?

DENISE. Oh, very *nice.*

TRISHA. You're sure?

DENISE. Oh, absolutely. Highly chic.

TRISHA. It's not too short?

DENISE. Just so. I mean, just very, very chic.

TRISHA. Chic, eh.

DENISE. That's right.

TRISHA, *in pleasure, does a little swirl, singing:*

TRISHA. Bye bye baby bye bye . . .

DENISE *rolls over, pours herself another Pernod.*
TRISHA *takes off the frock.*

DENISE. You know, you do –

TRISHA. Yuh, what?

DENISE. Look good. Looks great, on you.

Slight pause.

You wear it well.

TRISHA *looks at* DENISE, *not sure what she's implying.*

TRISHA. Oh. Yuh.

To change the subject:

Hey, meant to ask. The disco.

DENISE. Disco?

TRISHA. Yuh. How was it?

DENISE. Oh, all right.

TRISHA. All right?

DENISE. Well, great. Was lots of reggae.

TRISHA. Who was there?

DENISE. Oh, Sharon, Debbie, people.

TRISHA (*into a monkey imitation*). Huh-uh-uh.

DENISE. What you doing?

TRISHA. Them two. Half the time can't tell they're girls or blokes.

Monkey:

Huh-uh.

DENISE. Yuh, well.

Pause.

Talking of blokes –

TRISHA. Yuh?

DENISE. Gary there.

TRISHA. You what?

DENISE. Said, Gary there.

TRISHA *turns off the radio.*

TRISHA. Mean, *Gary*?

DENISE. Yuh, mean Gary. An' –

TRISHA. An' what?

DENISE. Well, in fact, he –

TRISHA *turns to* DENISE.

He's just a washout, Trish. Mean, not worth bothering. A real pain.

Pause.

Mean, not worth running after. Fact, you're better running opposite direction.

Pause.

Mean, Trish, even weedy Brian's –

TRISHA. How d'you know?

DENISE. Know what?

TRISHA. That he's a washout.

DENISE. Oh, cos of what happened.

TRISHA. Tell me what happened.

Pause.

DENISE. Well, like it all started, kind of joke, asked him to dance. You know, a kind of dare. And he was terrible. All eight left feet.

TRISHA. A kind of dare.

DENISE. That's right, and as it happened, smoochy number, dancing, tried to kiss me. Eight left hands an' all. A bleeding octopus. All fumbly. Mean, he tried to kiss me twice, an' missed me mouth both times.

Slight pause.

You ever had a nose-full someone's tongue? I mean, it made me want to sneeze, an' –

TRISHA. Den, you cow.

DENISE. You what.

TRISHA. You went with Gary.

DENISE. No I didn't.

TRISHA. Went with *Gary.*

DENISE. No, he went for me.

TRISHA. You cow.

DENISE. He's awful, Trish.

TRISHA. You, bloody cow.

DENISE. Stop calling me a cow.

TRISHA. Why not? It's what you are.

Pause.

DENISE. Trish, I was telling you cos of –

TRISHA. Not surprised he hit your nose.

DENISE. You what?

TRISHA. Could hardly miss it.

DENISE. Now, Trish –

TRISHA. Great big fat cow nose.

She is crying.

I'm not surprised he wouldn't kiss you properly. I mean, he probably just did it for a joke himself. Kiss Denny. Probably a bet. Kiss ugly Denny.

DENISE. What.

TRISHA. Like they all say.

DENISE *is looking, hard, at* TRISHA.
TRISHA *knocks over the Pernod bottle.*

Pernodd. Per – noh. Think you're so flash. So smart. When all they're doing's laughing cos no boy'd look at you.

Pause.

DENISE. If they're all like Gary, wouldn't want 'em to.

TRISHA (*sarcastic*). Oh, course you wouldn't would you?

DENISE. No.

Pause.

TRISHA. I think you better go.

DENISE. I will.

TRISHA. Right now.

DENISE. I will.

DENISE *stands.*
She looks at the notice-board.

I wouldn't want 'em to.

TRISHA. Just piss off out of it, Denise, OK?

DENISE. Them creeps. Them smutty little boys. Their gap-teeth, spots and pus. And think they're such big men, when stupid little teenies go an' scream at 'em.

She rips down a picture of the Bay City Rollers.
TRISHA *turns in horror, but doesn't dare to say anything or intervene.*

Them stupid teenies, dreaming one day one of 'em will fall for me, oh bliss, oh rapture, Love That Lasts For Ever And Your Whole Life's Changed. When all they really want's to get inside your pants and hump you.

She rips down the picture love story.

But still, spend all those hours, all that work, that *time.*

She's pulled down a beauty chart.

The money, fuck's sake, where you find it? Moisturizers, creams, mascara, powders, spotstick, lipstick, shadow, what the fuck's a blusher?, all this shit . . .

Screws up the cutting:

So a'n't you got a face?
Face of your own?

Slight pause.

Under all that shit, that waste, life of your own?

Pause.

TRISHA. My posters.

DENISE. Oh, your *posters*. Poor old *posters*.

Pause.

TRISHA. Den. Who's saying this to you.

DENISE. Miss Lockett says it. In our conversations.

Pause.

Conversations, that we have, together.

Pause.

Says that girls like you are just a waste of time.

Mocking:

'A'nt she got lovely shoes.'

Pause.

Well. Say *something*. Dear Patricia.

TRISHA *suddenly, very fast and angry*:

TRISHA. Yuh will, true what I said. All say you can't get boys. I can, they come here, come up here, my fellas, they all say to me, your best friend, Denny, Trisha, all my boys say, wouldn't touch her with a ten-foot pole. Or sometimes 20. Sometimes 20 foot, they wouldn't touch you with, that's what they say to me.

She screams:

MY BOYFRIENDS SAY TO ME.

Pause.

DENISE. Your boyfriends say.

She turns and goes out quickly.
Pause.

TRISHA. Oh Den.

Oh Den.

I'm sorry.

Blackout.

Scene Fourteen

Immediately, the title track from Suzie Quatro's 'Your Momma Won't Like Me'. During it, lights on the Youth Club. Two tables, each with four chairs. A bowl of sugar on only one of the tables. During the first verse and chorus, SHARON *and then* DEBBIE *enter, each with plastic cups of coffee.*

SHARON. Hi Deb.

DEBBIE. Hi Shar.

They look round, as the music goes on.
DENISE *enters. She too has a coffee.*

SHARON. Hi Den.

DENISE. Hi Deb. Hi Shar.

The three GIRLS *look round the room.*

SHARON. Well, shall we sit?

DEBBIE. Why not.

SHARON. Down here?

DENISE. OK.

They sit at the sugarless table, DEBBIE *and* SHARON *notice that* TRISHA *has appeared in the club, also carrying a plastic coffee.*

DEBBIE. Oh.

SHARON. Ah.

And cut the record, just before the second verse starts. DEBBIE, SHARON *and* DENISE *talk pointedly among themselves.*

SHARON. Well, see, we had this dare, a gang of us, the most could nick from Lipton's. So we all go in, and course I'm last, so get the most to nick. And I get lifted, check-out girl, they hauls me off, to see the manager.

DENISE. What happened then?

TRISHA moves nearer the table.

SHARON. Well, s'luck would have it, left alone with him. And he says, what's a nice young pretty girl like you . . . So I says, yuh, you're right, I am quite young and pretty, if you call the police I'll tell 'em that you was alone with me in here and tried a finger.

TRISHA. Hey, Den, look –

SHARON. Hey, girls, I didn't know was slag night. Did you Debbie?

DEBBIE. No, I didn't. Did you Den?

Slight pause.

DENISE. No, didn't know, was slag night.

SHARON. Shall we move?

SHARON and DEBBIE stand, DENISE *following, careful not to catch* TRISHA's *eyeline. They go to the other table and sit.*

DENISE (*nervy attempt at assurance*). So what d'he say?

SHARON. The Manager? Well, kind of spluttered, you know, say'n as how this time he'd let it go, but next time, you know. So I says, cos now this other bloke's come in, I says Oh Thank You Mr Manager. I'll never do anything like this again, I promise. And so off I goes. An' still got half a dozen sachets of shampoo stuffed down me trousers, i'n't I.

Slight pause, during which DENISE *gives a glance at* TRISHA *which* TRISHA *picks up, and, during the following,* TRISHA, *very carefully and nervously comes over.*

DEBBIE. But that wa'nt all.

SHARON. Oh, no. See we, we thought the check-out girl, like needed something of a caution, so as how she wouldn't do that kind of thing again.

TRISHA. Look, Den –

DEBBIE. Eh, Den, you know, that Karen Whitaker. She went with Barry Craig. An' what he did, he gave her phone number to all his mates. So she thought she was really popular. In fact, of course, all *knew*.

SHARON. Tring tring. Hur hur.

DEBBIE. Tring tring. Hur hur.

DENISE. Tring –

They look at her.

'Hallo. It's 4-3-7, double-5-4-3.'

It's TRISHA's *number. She goes rigid.*

DEBBIE. Well, shall we . . .

DEBBIE, SHARON *and* DENISE *get up and move back to the first table, leaving* TRISHA. TRISHA *sits.*

DENISE. So then, what happened? To the check-out girl?

SHARON. Oh, yuh, well. So we waits until she comes off, and just, you know, five or six of us, we jostles her. A bit. Down this side alley. Pushes her about. An' pulls her hair for her. Just, like, to caution her.

DEBBIE. Hey, Shar, remind me, wa'n't it that chair, over there, one slag's sat in, wa'n't that where Karen Whitaker was sitting, night we did her face in?

SHARON *quickly gets up, goes over to* TRISHA's *table. She stands there.* TRISHA *had just picked up her coffee to take a sip from it, and is stuck in terror.*

Uh – sugar?

TRISHA, *with her other hand, pushes the sugar bowl towards* SHARON. SHARON *picks it up.*

Ta, slag.

She turns back to return to the other table. TRISHA *is taking a sip of her coffee, as* SHARON, *suddenly, turns back and bangs the sugar back down on the table. This causes* TRISHA *to spill her coffee down herself.*

I'm on a diet, i'n I.

SHARON *back to the other table.*

'K, let's go. You coming Denny?

DENISE. Sure.

DEBBIE *and* DENISE *get up.*

DEBBIE (*to* DENISE, *as they go*). Was just a little jostle, see, Den, so as how she'd know.

The GIRLS *go out,* DENISE *trying hard not to look anywhere near* TRISHA. TRISHA *is left there, coffee dripping down her, crying. Music: The Shirelles: 'Will You Still Love Me Tomorrow'.*

Scene Fifteen

FRANCES'*s flat. The next day. It is in fact immediately before the first scene of the play. The poster book lies on the table in front of the sofa.*

No people on the set. As the record fades, the lights come up and with them the sound of typing.
ROSIE *and* FRANCES *call to each other from off, each side of the stage.*

ROSIE. Hey, Frankie!

FRANCES (*stop typing*). Yuh?

ROSIE. You ready?

FRANCES. In a *minute.*

ROSIE. What you doing?

FRANCES. Finishing some minutes.

Pause. Typing.

ROSIE. Frankie!

FRANCES (*stop typing*). Yuh?

ROSIE. These girls. You're sure they're competent?

FRANCES. Look, Rosie, do stop fussing 'bout those bloody children.

ROSIE. OK.

Pause. Typing.

ROSIE. Hey, Frankie!

FRANCES (*stop typing*). Yuh?

Bell.

ROSIE. I'll go.

ROSIE *crosses the stage.*
Typing continues
Then:

ROSIE. Hey, Frankie!

FRANCES. Yuh?

ROSIE. It's just the one! The other couldn't come!

FRANCES. OK!

Typing. TRISHA *comes in with* ROSIE.

ROSIE. So she couldn't come, then, your friend?

TRISHA *shakes her head.*

But you found the place all right?

TRISHA *nods.*

Well, good.

Slight pause.

Be with you in a minute, then.

ROSIE *goes out.* TRISHA *looks round. Then she sits on the sofa. The typing stops.*

FRANCES. Hey, Rosie?

ROSIE. Yuh?

FRANCES. What did it look like?

ROSIE. What did what what?

FRANCES. Did you think it looked like rain?

TRISHA *reaches for the book. Blackout and bring up Carole King. The record sticks, and swells.*

It might as well rain
It might as well rain
It might as well rain
It might as well rain

Scene Sixteen

The same. A couple of days later. It is earlier in the evening of Scene Two *of the play. The poster book is open on the table.* BREWER *stands there. He looks at the book.*

BREWER. Jesus Christ.

He shuts the book. FRANCES *enters, with a suitcase.*

FRANCES. Well, Mr Brewer.

BREWER. Ah. You off then?

FRANCES. Yes, I am off.

BREWER. On holiday.

FRANCES. Well, if you like.

BREWER. Abroad?

FRANCES. Why, should I?

Slight pause.
BREWER *smiles.*

BREWER. No.

FRANCES. No, not abroad. In fact my parents' place. They have this house in Suffolk. And I'm going there.

Slight pause.

I'm going home to mother.

BREWER. Yes.

Pause.

FRANCES. I mean, she'll live. I mean, it's not like manslaughter.

BREWER. I don't think anybody –

FRANCES. Don't they?

Pause.

BREWER. I think the HM thinks, it might be an idea, if you popped in for a chat. I think he feels it might be best, before you go away. Not so much because of, um, Patricia, as Denise.

Slight pause.

FRANCES. Oh, yes. The windows, in the science block.

BREWER. Indeed.

Pause.

The social worker feels that she – the messages that she received
– made her confused.

Pause.

Hence – Kristallnacht.

FRANCES. I see.

Slight pause.

Well, then. It's very kind of you –

BREWER (*suddenly*). You know, Frances, I'm sure you'll find this
hard to credit, but I did, once, long ago, believe that it was
possible to change those kids. To make them different, how I
thought they should be.

FRANCES. Well, bully for –

BREWER. And, just like you, I was appalled, disgusted with their
lives, their tatty fantasies, obsession with domestic and cosmetic
trivia, all that, and I tried to challenge them, disrupt them, force
them to see the poverty of their own vision of themselves.

But then I changed my mind. And why I changed it, and you'll
find this even harder to believe, the reason was my growing
feeling that it was a little, just a little arrogant on my part, to
think that I knew better what was good for them than they did.

And, you know, that what you've done, is you have taken from
those girls their props, supports, the things that hold up their
lives, and given nothing in return. You told them that they
shouldn't be their kind of person, and the only choice they had
was, on the one hand, for Denise, become a man, be what she
thought you wanted her to be, take on the toughness and
aggression, the machismo, be a thug, a bully-boy; and, on the
other hand, Patricia, cut off from her femininity, despise it, left
with nothing but despair. And I don't see, frankly, what else you
could think that they could do.

Pause.
With a slight, almost apologetic little smile:

Well, that's –

FRANCES *turns on* BREWER.

FRANCES. Do you – really – think I haven't thought – about *exactly* –

The sound of the door stops FRANCES.
Enter ROSIE.

ROSIE (*not sure of the situation*). Well, hallo.

BREWER (*stands*). Hallo. I'm Nick. Nick Brewer. Frances'
colleague.

ROSIE. Oh, I see.

BREWER. And, now, I think, perhaps I ought to –

FRANCES. Nick's been explaining, Rosie, how he views events.

ROSIE. Oh, has he?

FRANCES. Kindly popped round to put me right on human nature.

ROSIE. Nice of him.

FRANCES. And how to tamper with it's somehow to deform the
natural.

Pause.
BREWER *decides to go.*

BREWER. All right, I suppose, that I can understand, why you . . .

FRANCES. Can understand?

BREWER (*at the exit*). That's what I said.

FRANCES. You patronising shit.

Pause. BREWER *turns back.*

BREWER. All right. I won't be patronising. I'll say what I mean.

FRANCES. You do that.

BREWER. And what I *do* mean, Frances, is that frankly I don't
think, for you, this business has a thing to do with those two
girls.

FRANCES. You what?

BREWER. They're just a sideshow, and the star is you. And, no, I'm
not going to presume to even try and guess at why you see
yourself as Joan of Arc, what kink that is, what went wrong
when, but the result has been that you've transferred your
agonies and insecurities and pain on to two schoolgirls, and
what's happened is that you've destroyed them by your arrogant
conviction that their choices, what they've chosen as their lives,
their interests, their dreams, are worthy of contempt. And I hope

all the other girls, the Debbies and the Jackies and the Jo's, hope if they want nothing more than to be wives and mother they've chosen that, they'll realise that what you and your twisted sisters offer is a great deal less, because its content, despite all the rhetoric, is bitterness, self-hatred and despair.

BREWER *sees that* FRANCES *is crying.*

Oh, my God.

Pause.
BREWER *doesn't know what to do.*

ROSIE (*quietly*). When I was 19, I was asked to this wedding. And at the reception afterwards, met Howard. We stood near each other, giggled at the speeches, drank the fizzy wine. And then he asked me to go out with him, and I said yes, so out we went, and then he asked, well, in a month or so, if I would be engaged to him, and I said yes, and so engaged we were, and then before I knew it I was being asked if I would love and honour and obey, and I said yes, and love and honour and obey I did, and shortly after that I must have stopped the pill, cos I had Damion and three years later I had Sophie, complications and my tubes tied up, and I do not recall, throughout that happy fairy tale, one single, solitary choice at all. I never chose to get engaged. Be married. Have my children. I was chosen.

BREWER. Yes, well –

ROSIE. Now, you will know the concept of the Deja Vu. The feeling, I've done this, been here before. It's quite disturbing. Even more disturbing is the feeling that I had, from time to time, throughout my happy fairy life, a feeling in the night-time, in the darkness, of Non Deja Vu, a sense of loss of something that I should have been, but I hadn't, sense of never really doing, never thinking, anything; a sense of being thought and being done. Which you will doubtless find it hard to understand. Because, although there's limits to your choices, you can choose and map your life. Whereas, my life, and Trisha's, and Denise's, aren't like yours, because they are not mappable. They're mapped.

So don't you talk to me, to Frances or to them, about free choice. Cos, on that score, dear Nick, you just don't know you're born.

Pause.

BREWER. All I can say . . . is that a girl has tried to kill herself.

ROSIE. Oh *Christ* –

BREWER. Another girl has gone berserk, and, there, your friend is sitting on that sofa crying. They are all unhappy. Look at her. They are all miserable, their misery was caused by someone in this room, and I assure you that it wasn't me. Goodbye.

He goes out.
Pause.

ROSIE. Well, what a shit.

FRANCES. You think so?

ROSIE. Yes, of course. Don't you?

FRANCES. Don't know.

Pause.

You see, I told her that life was waste. Oh, not exactly. Not exactly in those words. What I said was, you can have a better life, tara tara, let me take you up the mountain, away from all of this, and I'll show you what it could be like. What I didn't realise was that the route, away from her own life, towards my gleaming fantasy, turned out to go through seven plateglass windows.

(*To* ROSIE.) Just don't know.

ROSIE. It wasn't wrong. It was right, to show her how it could be different. I mean, mean, surely, it was right to show her how her life could change.

(*Quite angry.*) I mean, for Christ's sake, Frankie, how can you say that it was wrong? How could you?

FRANCES *responds fast, with some aggression:*

FRANCES. You know, when *I* was 15, I remember, was the same as poor old Trisha. Yes, I used to think, like she did, when I met him at the candy store, and when he whispered sweet and secret nothings in my ear, and when we walked off hand in hand into the sunset, that in that very moment, suddenly my whole life changed.

But still, the thing was, I did know, p'raps unlike Trisha, deep down, that the whole shebang was so much shit. It wouldn't last. The blissful moment was, by definition, just momentary.

But when I was 19, and went to college, 1968, the dawn in

which of course 'twas bliss to be alive, and when I met him at
the demo and he whispered sweet and secret dialectics in my ear,
and when we walked off hand in hand into the sit-in, and in *that*
very moment, suddenly my whole life changed . . .

I thought it had.

And even more, I needed to believe *that* tatty teenage fantasy was
going to be a blueprint for The Changing Of The World.

It's simple. Thought we could change people. We were wrong.

And so, friend Rosie, I am going home.

ROSIE. Frances. Don't go.

FRANCES *stands and goes to her suitcase.*

FRANCES. Back home. Where I'll be safe.

ROSIE. Stay here. At least a day or two.

FRANCES *picks up her case.*

FRANCES. Returning back, where I belong. Back to the past.
Because I like it there.

*She remembers she's forgotten something. She snaps her fingers. Puts
down her case, goes out.*

ROSIE. Speak for yourself. Friend Frances.

A moment. FRANCES *re-enters. She has sunglasses.*

FRANCES. Sunglasses.

ROSIE. Look, Frankie.

FRANCES. Mm?

ROSIE. Look, Frankie, I just feel I ought to say . . .

FRANCES. Go on.

ROSIE. That I know why you believe the things you do.

Pause.

FRANCES. Well, I must own that, at times like these, that's more
than I –

ROSIE. Because, when you were small, you told me. You could
speak of little else. And I remember – how your eyes would
blaze.

Pause.

FRANCES. Well, now. How does it go? When I was a child . . . I
spoke as a child, but when . . . I can't remember how it ends.
Something about growing up, and you can't be childish any
more. St Paul. In One Corinthians.

She makes to go, then turns back.

You see, the *real* mistake, was thinking that that need, the need
to think those things, was a rational decision. To convince oneself
that one had woken up, one morning, had a glance in the mirror,
and *decided, seen*, that all of history's the struggle of the classes,
fancy that, that capital creates the means of its own overthrow,
of course, that, well I never, there appears to be this
contradiction between the social methods of production and the
private ownership of capital, well glory be, and all those rational
cosmetics, smeared in layers across that sad and lonely, desperate
little face that I had seen, that morning, in the mirror. Blueprint,
change the world.In fact, a blueprint to escape the world. And
me. And I've been on the run, from me, this seven years, and
now at last I'm going to turn me in.

I'm sorry we were wrong.

She goes out. ROSIE *left alone. Then,* ROSIE *takes a decision, and
follows* FRANCES *out.*

Scene Seventeen

Music fades, and lights on a hospital ward. TRISHA *sits on her bed.*
ROSIE *stands there, carrying a leatherbound book which she gives to*
TRISHA.
    TRISHA *looks at the book.*

ROSIE. I brought you this.

TRISHA. Oh, yuh.

ROSIE. A book, by Charlotte Bronte.

TRISHA. Thanks.

Pause.

ROSIE. How are you feeling, then?

TRISHA.Well.

Rubbing her tummy, ruefully.

Bit better.

ROSIE. Yuh. Have they been nice to you? The nurses and the doctors?

TRISHA. Yuh. Been fine.

Pause.

The sister said, it wasn't natural. Like what I did. A girl like me. A pretty girl.

ROSIE. Well, you are very pretty.

TRISHA *a slight smile at* ROSIE.

TRISHA. Mm.

Pause.

S'true about Denise? Went mad, and smashing things?

ROSIE. I think that she felt guilty.

TRISHA. Oh. She would.

ROSIE. I'm sorry . . .?

TRISHA. Oh just always . . . F'I'd been there . . .

ROSIE. Yes? What?

TRISHA. She wouldn't have. (*Pause.*) I'm pleased you came.

ROSIE. Well, I was glad to.

Pause.

TRISHA *nods.*

I know she'd want me to, send all her very best. Because she cares so much, for both of you.

Pause. TRISHA *bites her lip.*

TRISHA. Mm. Well.

Pause. ROSIE, *decision*:

Look, Trisha.

TRISHA. Hm?

ROSIE. Just don't – forget it. Write it off. Just don't, pretend it never happened. You might feel, must feel that everything has stopped, but that's not true. What's happening is that you're changing, and that isn't good or bad, but just – it's true.

I mean, the feeling, carnage. Feeling smashed and broken. That is what change feels like. You are feeling change.

You see?

Pause.

TRISHA. I s'pose so.

TRISHA *troubled. She turns away from* ROSIE. *She sees her mirror, picks it up.*

You know perhaps she's right. The nurse. It isn't natural. A girl like me.

TRISHA *looks at* ROSIE:

So what else can I do?

DENISE *has entered. She has a big bottle of Pernod.*

DENISE. Uh. Trish.

She gives a silly wave.

TRISHA. Oh, Den. Oh, Miss. Oh, this is Den.

Pause.

My friend.

ROSIE. I sort of gathered.

She smiles, stands and goes.
DENISE *goes to* TRISHA.

DENISE. Oh, Trish. You silly cow.

TRISHA. Oh, Den. You silly cow.

A moment. Then DENISE *affectionately mocking*:

DENISE. 'So what else can I do?'

Scene Eighteen

The music fades, as soft, warm lights fade up on the terrace of a big house in Suffolk. It is early evening on a beautiful September day, in 1975. The terrace furniture, including, perhaps a rocking chair, is old, good, bleached by the sun. Perhaps the odd old and well-used wooden toy. Certainly a rather battered ball.

COLIN *stands on the terrace. He carries a rucksack. He puts it down. He takes off his jacket. He stands there, enjoying the sun.*

FRANCES *enters, from the house, with two whiskies. She is dressed, comfortably, in shorts and a tee-shirt. It is important that her clothes are sufficiently ageless that similar clothes could be worn by a teenager 14 years before.*

FRANCES. Well, this is it.

She hands COLIN *his drink.*

COLIN. So, this is how the other half . . .

FRANCES. That's right.

Pause.

COLIN. So where are they? Your people.

FRANCES. They're in Crete.

She sits.

COLIN. It is, the view is really beautiful.

FRANCES. I love this place.

COLIN *sits.*

COLIN. So what you been doing with yourself, all summer long?

FRANCES. Oh, very little. Being waited on. And playing with my nephews and my nieces. Going walkies. Lying in the sweet and sticky, British middle-class embrace.

They are, in many ways, quite wonderful.

And seeing no one. From my other life. Reading no pamphlets. Engaging in no polemics or critiques.

Brightly:

And I haven't had a fuck for three months. You have no idea how comforting the celibate existence can be.

How's, who is it, Sarah?

COLIN. I don't know.

Slight pause.

It is quite, restful, as you say.

Slight pause.

Won't last.

FRANCES. Why not?

COLIN. I've got a job. Been offered, rather. Which will be, if I take it, quite the opposite of restful.

FRANCES. What is it?

COLIN. With Granada. Want to do a series, for the 50th anniversary next year.

Slight pause.

FRANCES. The anniversary of what?

COLIN. The General Strike.

FRANCES. Ah, yes. Researching?

COLIN. And presenting part of it.

FRANCES. Colin is giving up humble pedagogy to concentrate full-time on his mediastar career?

Pause.

COLIN. Yes, well. I think it's still important. For today.

FRANCES. Oh, yes, indeed.

Pause.

So raise the curtain. Lights and music. Yet another in our series of Great Moments that went wrong. Nine days that nearly shook the world. May Days that weren't.

COLIN. You what?

FRANCES. Oh, just a theory. That I have.

Pause.

COLIN. Do you think that I should take it?

FRANCES. There's a question?

COLIN. Yes. Of course there is.

Pause.

My contact, on the programme, is approximately thirty. Works, in average, a 12-hour day. Commutes, by train or plane, from Golden Square to Manchester. Oh, he's a thrusting fellow, as they all are, thrusting and ambitious, eyes are never still, but darting round, to check who's up, who's down, who's out. And so they make their programmes, radical, progressive, calling for the overthrow of capital and for the building of a world of cooperation and solidarity, with a zeal, a lust for competition that would make the Soviet Olympic team look positively lackadaisical. And playing out a permanent audition. In the late night restaurants, and passing round the dry white wine, and dry white liberated ladies, from research, from hand to hand. Like relay batons.

So there has to be a question, if I want to join that Conga. Doesn't there.

Pause. End of confession. He stands.

Well. You want another?

FRANCES *looks at* COLIN.

FRANCES. Oh, deal Col. Dear Peter Pan.

COLIN. You what?

FRANCES. Oh, just. I'm sorry. What I called you, night I threw you out.

You have – this quite amazing innocence. This sense of, well, you always look surprised. At what is, let's be honest, pretty obvious.

Pause.

COLIN. I see.

With a slight smile:

Well, one could ask – If I am Peter Pan. Who have I come to visit, in her Wendy House.

Pause.

I'll get the drinks.

COLIN *goes into the house. Pause. Then* FRANCES *snaps her fingers.*

FRANCES. When I became a man, I put away childish things.

She laughs.

Oh, dear. Again. An axiom that seems not to apply.

Pause.

Dear Col. Dear me. With all these vipered bosoms. All these Wendy Houses, dreamy Suffolks, Golden Squares.

Why do we still . . .

Pause.
FRANCES *puts her feet up on the chair. She puts her arms round her knees. She looks, suddenly, very much younger.*
And we notice that the lights are changing. Instead of the warmth of the evening, it's a dazzling high summer afternoon.

And ROSIE *tiptoes in behind* FRANCES. ROSIE *is dressed in shorts and a T-shirt. She – and* FRANCES – *are 13 years old. It is the summer of 1961.* ROSIE *puts her hands over* FRANCES' *eyes. A little struggle and quite a lot of giggling follows.*

ROSIE. They're gone.

FRANCES. All day. To Lowestoft.

ROSIE. To see your rich aunt. Your very very rich relations.

FRANCES. Stop it. Where have you been?

ROSIE. I went swimming. In your very very nice expensive swimming pool.

Pause.

FRANCES. I didn't know you could swim.

ROSIE. Hidden depths.

She 'swims'.

I didn't like to with your family.

Pause.

D'you think they like me?

FRANCES. Yes of course.

ROSIE. Don't think your dad does much.

FRANCES. Well I don't like him much.

ROSIE (*imitation; plummy voice*). 'Now shake a leg there Rosie.'

FRANCES (*imitation*). 'Top of the morning then old girl.'

ROSIE (*imitation*). 'Well if it isn't Frankie's little friend.'

They roll about.

FRANKIE (*imitation*). 'So what's your poison, Rosie?'

ROSIE (*imitation*). 'Well, I'll drink to that.'

FRANKIE *picks up the ball and tosses it.* ROSIE *catches it. They play with the ball. Finally,* ROSIE *stuffs the ball up her T-shirt. They giggle. The laughter subsides.*

FRANKIE. Are . . . you . . . going to have a baby?

ROSIE. I should think so. Yes.

FRANKIE. How many?

ROSIE. I told my mum I was going to have eight.

FRANKIE. That's quite a lot.

ROSIE. She said that I'd soon change my tune.

FRANKIE. Sometimes I'm not sure if we should.

Pause. ROSIE *is rolling the ball under her hand.*

ROSIE. Mm?

FRANKIE. With you know. If they're going to blow the world up anyway.

ROSIE *rolls the ball under her hand and lifts it high. She turns it.*

ROSIE. I turn ze vorld.

Pause.

I run ze vorld.

FRANKIE. Just for a day.

ROSIE *throws the ball to* FRANKIE. *They play with the ball.* FRANKIE *finds the ball in front of her crutch. She holds it there and giggles.* ROSIE *giggles.*

Do you wish you'd been a boy?

ROSIE. I think my dad does.

FRANKIE. But do you?

ROSIE. Nar.

A game developing.

Hey can you do backstroke?

FRANKIE. Backstroke? Yes of course.

ROSIE. And breast-stroke?

FRANKIE *and* ROSIE *doing the breast-stroke on the bench.*

FRANKIE. Sure. (*She 'swims'.*) I'm going to be sick . . .

ROSIE. And butterfly?

It becomes very energetic. In the midst of it all:

FRANKIE. I must I must

ROSIE. – improve my . . .

They fall back exhausted in the backstroke position. Their heads are upside down.

FRANCES. Hey. Do you think about the future?

She's pronounced it 'foocher'.

ROSIE. What, the flowers?

FRANCES (*silly*). No, the fu-ture. What will Chance to Come To Pass.

ROSIE. Not much. I mean, I don't think about it much. Not very very much.

FRANCES. I do.

Pause.

I wonder. What d'you think we'll be like in ten years time.

ROSIE. Dunno.

They change position.

ROSIE. I think we'll still be friends.

FRANKIE. Do you?

ROSIE. Oh yes. I'm sure.

Pause.

FRANKIE. Is that a promise?

ROSIE. Yuh. A promise.

FRANKIE. Cross your heart and hope to die?

Pause.

ROSIE. 'I'll drink to that.'

Pause. A questioning look.

Hey. Can we?

Pause.

FRANKIE. Yes. Why not. Go on.

ROSIE goes out to raid the drinks cupboard. COLIN enters with drinks. The lights are changing back to the September evening.

COLIN. Well, I must say, your dad's well stocked.

FRANCES (*taking her drink*). Oh, yes. He is.

As the lights have changed fully.

He's excellently stocked.

COLIN *sits.*

FRANCES. You know, I think I'm going back.

COLIN. Back where?

FRANCES. Back home.

COLIN. Is this not home?

FRANCES. Oh, no.

Pause.

I've passed the point, of no return. The Wendy House was smashed, oh, long ago.

Pause.

She jumps up, quite brightly, going towards the house, and turning back to COLIN.

So. Back. To all the mess and muck and guilt and failure and missed opportunity. Remembering, perhaps, occasionally, what all that pain is for.

So what else can I do?

COLIN *and* FRANCES *look at each other.*

Bring in Vivaldi's 'Winter'.

Scene Nineteen

FRANCES *stays there.* COLIN *goes. Enter* TRISHA *and* DENISE. *They are grown-ups now. And* ROSIE *enters, in adult clothes, with a wrap for* FRANCES, *as the music fades.*

TRISHA. She'd always been the dreamy one, forever longing for the one true love that would transport her into endless bliss.

FRANCES. So perhaps it was predictable that she'd get married to an up-and-coming chap in chips, and settle down.

ROSIE. And as soon as she clocked that his eye was wandering, she saw to it that she got pregnant pronto, and now she and Emma live on alimony and are blissfully content.

DENISE. She'd always been the do-or-die type, full of madcap notions, wild ideas and harebrained schemes.

FRANCES. And so maybe it wasn't much of a surprise when having quite dramatically failed a tranche of O levels, she was picked up by this bloke who took her first to London, then New York –

ROSIE. Where, via a number of adventures, she became an action painter with an arts and crafts collective off Canal St called Gynocracy.

RUTH *has entered.*

FRANCES. And *she* had always liked the writing.

RUTH. And so those who'd known her weren't too shocked to learn that she had penned a 'witty, bitter and astringent' –

ROSIE. But essentially romantic novel,

FRANCES. Well, essentially of the *genre* –

ROSIE. Which had been eagerly received by the public and the critics.

RUTH. Even though some feminist reviewers weren't quite sure how to read its tone.

FRANCES. But most importantly, for her, the book provoked a shoal of letters, from the past.

TRISHA. Dear Miss, we never knew you were an *author.*

DENISE. Miss, you never let on you wrote books.

RUTH. Dear Frances, I'm not sure if you'll recall –

FRANCES. All of which were full of quite the most surprising if not downright shocking news.

TRISHA. In fact, miss, I got work, with an employment agency. I give advice, like to young people, on pursuing a career.

DENISE. In fact, miss, I got pregnant. By an accident. And me and Josephine, we jumped the list, and got this flat.

TRISHA. And I like it cos of what they say. The ideas that they come up with, about what they want to do. I mean, they call 'em stupid, and fantastical. But I say, well, you may be right, but it's as good a place as any to begin.

DENISE. And I like it cos we got self-management, and it's muggins who gets sent down to the council – as the loudmouth one sez *they* – about things like the rubbish and the lifts and how this patch of land we got behind the flats we could use for allotments, place for things to grow.

RUTH. And in fact, I dropped out of sociology. And dropped the squatting too. And my lover got this offer, a sabbatical in Oregon. But I decided not to go, but to stay and drop back in.

And took a course. Of all things, in accountancy.

And now it's mainly mainstream stuff. But there's still some clients, co-ops, and collectives, a partnership of women plumbers, still a magazine or two. All in a state of utter shambles. All in most urgent need of auditorial first aid.

But I won't let my partners touch 'em. 'Cos they're mine.

ROSIE. And Rosie lived with Frances, and off Howard, and spent her evenings planning strenuous and rather special holidays down rivers and up mountains and resolved that she would never cook again.

TRISHA. And Trisha tried to match her clients' wishes to their needs.

DENISE. While Denise emerged as all-in-all a most superior class of mother.

FRANCES. And – and Frances wrote their dreams.

Pause. We begin to hear the Vivaldi again.

DENISE. And little did they think.

TRISHA. And who'd have thought,

RUTH. And how could anyone have known . . .

FRANCES. That their dreams would stand them all in such good stead in the times that were to come.

The WOMEN *look at each other. A moment.*
The Music swells, and the lights fade.

Our Own People

Our Own People was first presented by Pirate Jenny at the Half Moon Theatre and on tour, in November 1977, with the following cast:

BARONESS COCKBURN, Inquiry Chair	Victoria Plum
JILL WATTS, Barrister	Sue Glanville
MANSUR HUSSEIN, Committee Chair	Tariq Yunus
MUHAMMAD LATEEF, Interpreter	Reggee Ranjha
SAVITRI BHANDARI, Committee Member	Indira Joshi
HAMEED FARUQI, Shop Steward	Tariq Yunus
RANJIT SINGH SANDHU, Committee	Regee Ranjha
GEORGE JOWETT, General Secretary	John Gillett
FRANK KITCHEN, Senior Steward	Malcolm Raeburn
JOAN DAWSON, Shop Steward	Chrissue Cotteril
NICHOLAS CLIFFORD, Barrister	Malcolm Raeburn
ERIC HARPER, Managing Director	John Gillett
ASHUYA RIDLEY, Conciliation Officer	Indira Joshi
A MIDDLE AGED WOMAN	Victoria Plum
A YOUNG PAKISTANI	Reggee Ranjha
AN OFFICIAL	Malcolm Raeburn

Directed by Walter Donahue
Designed by Di Seymour
Lighting designed by Eddie Heron
Stage Managed by Sue Lovett

Our Own People is based round a fictional industrial dispute in Yorkshire in the 1970s. A chronology of the events of this dispute is included as an appendix to the text of the play.

Scene One

The Court.

Enter CHAIR, WATTS, CLIFFORD, JOWETT, HUSSEIN, LATEEF, BHANDARI *and* DAWSON.

DAWSON. In the late spring and early summer of 1975, there was a strike at a weaving mill in Beckley, a small textile town near Bradford in Yorkshire.

BHANDARI. It wasn't a very big dispute. The firm employed under 200 people, less than half of whom came out on strike.

HUSSEIN. What made this strike special, however, was that all the strikers were Asians, and nearly all the people who stayed at work were white.

HUSSEIN *sits.*

LATEEF. The strike began as a dispute over pay, but it soon escalated into a bitter conflict over the treatment of Asian workers by the company, the union, and their fellow employees. Pickets were mounted, and several ugly incidents took place.

LATEEF *sits.*

CLIFFORD. In the seventh week of the strike, the Department of Employment set up a Court Of Inquiry to investigate the affair. At the Inquiry, the company, Darley Park Mills Ltd, was represented by Nicholas Clifford, Barrister-at-law. Mr Clifford had made his name defending companies before the Monopolies' Commission.

CLIFFORD *sits.*

JOWETT. The National Union of Weavers was represented by George Jowett, its General Secretary, Mr Jowett was noted in Trade Union circles for his vigorous advocacy of selective import controls.

JOWETT *sits.*

WATTS. The strikers' case was put by Jill Watts, another Barrister. Mrs Watts, who had been involved in a variety of radical causes, agreed to accept the brief for a nominal fee.

WATTS *sits.*

CHAIR. The Court of Inquiry was chaired by the Baroness Cockburn, a former junior Minister who was elevated to the peerage after Labour's defeat in 1970. Baroness Cockburn, a director of the BBC and a prospective member of the Equal Opportunities Commission, was also presently chairing the Royal Commission on River Pollution in England and Wales.

CHAIR *sits.*

BHANDARI. The Inquiry was held in the Mechanics Institute, Beckley.

DAWSON. It took place on the third and fourth of July, 1975.

Exit DAWSON *and* BHANDARI. *The* CHAIR *introduces the Inquiry.*

CHAIR. Good morning, ladies and gentlemen. This is the opening of the Inquiry. My name is Ruth Cockburn and I am an independent person appointed by the Secretary of State for Employment with the following terms of reference:
'To inquire into the causes and circumstances of the present dispute between employees of the Darley Park Mills Company Ltd, and their employer, and to report'.

The Secretary of State has not laid down any specific rules of procedure and I can therefore decide the ground-rules we shall adopt. I don't intend to permit cross-examination, but questions can be asked through the chair at my discretion. The Inquiry will be in public, but we can go into camera if I feel it's necessary. There will be no evidence on oath and I want proceedings to be as informal as possible.

That's all I wish to say by way of introduction. I shall now ask Mrs Watts to open proceedings for the Strike Committee.

WATTS. Madam Chairman, the Strike Committee welcomes the chance to put its case to you, a case which is, I believe, one for simple justice. The strikers feel that they have been discriminated against by the company in terms of pay, conditions of work, and promotion. They have tried to resolve their grievances peacefully, and only as a last resort have they gone on strike. I intend to ask the strikers, as far as possible, to present their own case to you. But I feel it would be helpful to give a brief summary of the dispute, which my witnesses will as it were flesh out in their evidence. I shall be making a number of general points about arrangements at the Mill, and if I make any errors of fact I trust that the other parties will intervene.

CHAIR. I'm sure you will make no mistakes, Mrs Watts, and I am equally sure that if you do so, they will be corrected.

WATTS. Darley Park Mills employs nearly 200 workers. Just over half of them are employed as yarn-preparers, cloth-menders, and in general labouring and clerical capacities. The 90 or so actual weavers are concerned with overseeing the weaving machines.

There are, however, two major dividing lines between the weavers, which lie at the heart of this dispute. The first concerns the job itself. On any one shift, there are two types of weaver; ordinary weavers, who look after a certain number of looms, and a smaller number of time-weavers, who are in general more experienced and who assist weavers when they cannot solve a particular problem. The time-weavers are so-called because they are paid on a fixed-rate basis, which works out at between £5 and £10 more than the ordinary weavers' piecework earnings.

CHAIR. Can you give us rough proportions?

WATTS. Well, on an average shift of say 20 ordinary weavers, there'd be four time-weavers.

CHAIR. About one in five. Thank you.

WATTS. The other major division between the weavers is the machines they work. Since the early 1970s, the company has been scrapping its old Dobcross looms and replacing them with new Sultzer weaving machines. This process has now been half-completed. The weavers on the new machines work a rotating, three-shift system, and are therefore all men –

CHAIR. Forgive me, this is because of legal restrictions on women working nights?

WATTS. That's right, whereas the Dobcross operation is still two-shift, and does employ women on days. There is, therefore, a permanent nightshift on the old looms.

CHAIR. Again, can we have the rough proportions?

WATTS. Yes, indeed. On the Dobcross dayshift, there are about 25 women, including eleven Asian women. The Dobcross nightshift is, of course, all men, of whom the vast majority are Asian. There are about 40 Sultzer weavers, including about half a dozen Asians. That is the general position now.

CHAIR. Perhaps before you go on, Mrs Watts, we had better just double-check that everyone is in agreement thus far, and then we can take it as read. I'm sure there can be no basic –

CLIFFORD. Well, there is one point, Madam Chairman –

CHAIR. I spoke too soon. Mr Clifford.

CLIFFORD. It's really whether we want to discuss the transfer of machinery at this point. Obviously this is going to come up again later, but we could clear it up now.

CHAIR. I think it might be better to leave it until it comes up of its own accord.

CLIFFORD. Very well.

CHAIR. Mrs Watts.

WATTS. Thank you. The dispute began, in fact, with a complaint about bonus payments among the Dobcross nightshift weavers. However, this grievance as it were exposed a number of other grievances, about the treatment of Asian women on the dayshift, and, more importantly, the whole question of whites and Asians having equal opportunities for promotion to time-weaving posts. Through the union, the Asians presented all these grievances to management, and having failed to get any satisfaction, the Asian workers came out on strike on the 16th of May.

Because all the strikers were Asian, the company invited a conciliation officer from the Manchester Community Relations Council, Anshuya Ridley, to mediate. An agreement was reached, and the first strike ended on the 28th.

CHAIR. For everyone's information, Mrs Ridley will be available to give evidence tomorrow.

WATTS. When the strikers returned, however, they found that two time-weaving vacancies had been filled by white workers while they had been out. The Asians viewed this as a breach of the spirit of the agreement and came out on strike again. Since then, the strikers have been sacked, and the dispute has been made official.

The only other major event, Madam Chairman, was the acceptance by the nonstriking workers of a redundancy and productivity scheme presented by the management three weeks ago. Because this meant that the company could not guarantee to take back all the striking workers, a solution of the dispute had been impossible to reach, and the present stalemate solution has continued to the present time.

I should now like to call the chairman of the strike Committee. I should mention that Mansur Hussein intends to give his evidence in English, but we have an interpreter to assist him should that prove necessary.

CHAIR. I'm happy with that.

WATTS. Mr Hussein, how long have you worked with the company, and in what capacity?

HUSSEIN. I have been employed since 1970, on the nightshift, in old looms.

WATTS. Could you explain the overtime position?

HUSSEIN. Well, there was a basic shift, but often we were told to work up to 12 hours.

WATTS. This was compulsory? You were told to do it and you did it?

HUSSEIN. Yes.

WATTS. Were you happy with this situation, initially?

HUSSEIN *looks at* LATEEF.

LATEEF (*in Urdu*). Initially.

HUSSEIN. Oh, yes. It was work. And with overtime, better money.

WATTS. What made you become less happy?

HUSSEIN. Well, for various reasons, I didn't wish to work nights all the time, and not to know when overtime would be.

WATTS. Can you say what the various reasons were?

HUSSEIN. Mostly, I got married.

CHAIR. I think that is as near as we are likely to get to the perfect answer.

WATTS. Indeed. Wasn't it also true that the pay became less attractive?

HUSSEIN. Yes. When I began, there was a differential bonus on permanent nights of about 15 per cent. By now it is – (*He speaks to* LATEEF *in Urdu*.) Reduced to?

LATEEF. Eroded.

HUSSEIN. Is eroded to about only five or six per cent.

WATTS. And that was your first basic demand, to have that differential restored, put back?

HUSSEIN. That is so.

WATTS. Thank you. I want to deal with promotion now. Almost all the nightshift workers are Asian. Has there ever been an Asian time-weaver on the shift?

HUSSEIN. Well, only one. The rest have been white. The one was appointed two years ago.

WATTS. Can you tell me how that appointment was made?

HUSSEIN. Yes. There was a vacancy, and the company appointed a white, who had worked on Sultzers. We indicated that we thought it should be an Asian from the shift.

WATTS. When you say 'indicated'?

HUSSEIN. We stopped working.

WATTS. Yes. And then?

HUSSEIN. Well, they caved in, and we started working again. They made an Asian a time-weaver.

CHAIR. Sorry, this was in addition to the other new one?

HUSSEIN. Yes.

WATTS. Now, Mr Hussein, I'd like to come to the build-up to the strike itself. How did you pursue your grievances?

HUSSEIN. Well, for a long time we have been trying to talk to Mr Kitchen.

WATTS. Mr Kitchen is the senior shop steward?

HUSSEIN. Yes, and we had some meetings with him, but very little seemed to be happening. We became quite frustrated, in fact. And so we wrote to Mr Jowett.

WATTS. What happened then?

HUSSEIN. Well, we had a meeting with Mr Kitchen, and Mr Jowett. And they wrote to management with our demands.

WATTS. And what was management's response?

HUSSEIN. Well, there was a meeting, and they turned down our demands. Two days later, we asked Mr Jowett to give strike notice and they wrote to management. A week later, we saw Mr Kitchen and asked him what had happened and he said nothing. We said we would come out on strike, but he said we must wait till we see Mr Jowett, who we met on Friday the 16th. He told us not to strike.

WATTS. He had given strike notice but he advised you not to strike?

HUSSEIN. That's right.

WATTS. So what did you do?

HUSSEIN. We set up our own committee and came out.

WATTS. Lastly, Mr Hussein, I'd like to deal with the agreement the strikers reached for a return to work, 12 days later, the deal reached with Mrs Ridley's assistance. In broad terms, could you describe it?

HUSSEIN. Well, the most important point was that there should be equality in promotion, between Asians and whites, to time-weaving jobs.

WATTS. Yes. And was there an agreement on the nightshift bonus?

HUSSEIN. Yes, there was a – um – (*To* LATEEF, *in urdu.*) Interim?

LATEEF. Interim.

HUSSEIN. Oh, yes, interim bonus for nights.

WATTS. Why only interim?

HUSSEIN. Well, because the idea was that the firm should finish phasing out the Dobcrosses quickly, and transfer everyone to Sultzers, so there would be no more permanent nights problem.

WATTS. And on the basis of that agreement, you returned to work on Wednesday 28th May.

HUSSEIN. Yes. And then we found –

WATTS. Forgive me, Mr Hussein. I'll be dealing with what you found, with the next witness. That's all I have at this stage.

CHAIR. I have only one question. You said 'We came out' on the 16th. Who was 'we' at this stage? I mean, who was on strike?

HUSSEIN. Well, all the nightshift, almost, some of the dayshift, and some of the Sultzer people. Also a few labourers and menders and so on.

CHAIR. I have to ask if all the strikers were Asian.

HUSSEIN. Yes.

CHAIR. And a large number of them, I mean, the Sultzer people and the non-weavers, had nothing to do with the dispute?

HUSSEIN. Not directly, no.

CHAIR. So can I ask you why they joined the strike?

Pause.

HUSSEIN. They joined the strike because it is normal that when there is a dispute in a factory everyone is involved. That is normal even when people are not directly affected. Or that is what we thought.

Lights change.

Scene Two

CHAIR, WATTS, JOWETT, CLIFFORD.

WATTS. Madam Chairman, before my next witness, as the issue of the phasing out and the Sultzer transfer has come into the story, perhaps we could deal with it now.

CHAIR. Thank you, Mrs Watts. Mr Clifford, perhaps you could explain all this.

CLIFFORD. Yes, Madam Chairman. As Mrs Watts correctly pointed out, Darley Park Mills is about half-way through a process of transferring from old Dobcross looms to new Sultzer weaving machines.

CHAIR. This is a general technological development that has been going on throughout the industry?

CLIFFORD. It is indeed. The Sultzer machines are much more competitive in many ways. It requires less pre-preparation of materials, it's faster, and requires less staff. In general, one weaver minds four Dobcrosses, but the same weaver can cope with eight Sultzers.

There are, however, fairly obvious redundancy implications. Any firm would want union agreement, but in this case it was imperative, because there is a Government grant-aid scheme for firms undertaking the transfer, and written union agreement is a condition of assistance.

CHAIR. When did this scheme begin?

CLIFFORD. In 1971. In effect, the company reached agreement with the union at that stage, but the union withdrew from the arrangement in 1973.

CHAIR. Perhaps Mr Jowett could explain why.

JOWETT. Well, basically Madam Chairman, the initial agreement was mainly concerned with female redundancies. We agreed on a programme of early retirement, natural wastage and other forms of voluntary de-manning –

CHAIR. I'm not sure 'de-manning' is quite the right expression under the circumstances.

JOWETT. Well, de-womaning or de-personing or whatever. There were some blokes involved as well. In any event, in 1973, the company came back and said that all this hadn't reduced the labour force by a sufficient amount, and that they'd have to sack a few. We refused this, and the company said it couldn't afford to continue the transfer under those circumstances.

CHAIR. Would the company accept this?

CLIFFORD. Well, more or less. In fact, the union took a generally much more belligerent line in 1973.

CHAIR. By 'belligerent' you mean that the union drove a hard bargain in 1973, whereas management had done rather well in 1971?

CLIFFORD. Well, yes. In fact, on the first agreement, there were really no strings attached at all.

CHAIR. A splendid deal.

CLIFFORD. It sometimes happens, Madam Chairman.

CHAIR. I really ought to let Mr Jowett comment on this. His reputation is at stake.

JOWETT. Well, you win some and you lose some. In '71 the industry was in recession, and I suppose we accepted things we wouldn't take in a boom year like '73. There's a bit of a fatalistic feeling in this industry, you know, that each downturn'll be the last. It's not, of course, or else we'd not be here.

CHAIR. So we can say that the transfer was as it were frozen in the 1973 position?

CLIFFORD. Yes. The situation remained the same until this year, when the company was forced to reopen the question.

CHAIR. Why 'forced'?

CLIFFORD. Well, frankly, because the government's grant-aid scheme stops next year.

CHAIR. That, as they say, figures.

CLIFFORD. The company re-opened negotiations in April. They were in progress when the present trouble broke out.

CHAIR. I'm sorry, I'm confused. I thought Mrs Ridley had recommended that the transfer question should be reopened at the end of the first strike, as part of the deal for a return to work. Were negotiations already in progress at that time?

CLIFFORD. They were. I think Mrs Ridley's point was that they should be pursued with vigour.

CHAIR. I see. I have only two more questions: first, can you give approximate figures on the weaving workforce in 1971, and when the transfer is complete?

CLIFFORD. Yes, I think so . . . Yes. There were 121 weavers in 1971. The projected figure is just over 60.

CHAIR. And finally, Mr Clifford, following that, the company did present a new scheme to the workforce during the second strike? A new scheme that was similar to the one they'd rejected in 1973?

CLIFFORD. Yes, the company did so. This new scheme was, I must confess somewhat to the company's surprise, overwhelmingly accepted by the non-striking workers on the 18th of June.

CHAIR. Thank you.

Lights change.

Scene Three

The Court.

CHAIR, WATTS, BHANDARI, LATEEF, CLIFFORD, JOWETT.

WATTS. My next witness is Savitri Bhandari. Mrs Bhandari, when did you start working at the mill.

BHANDARI. In 1973.

WATTS. You had in fact come to England from Uganda in 1972?

BHANDARI. Yes.

WATTS. Where did you work in the mill?

BHANDARI. I was on the Dobcross dayshift.

WATTS. Now, I want mainly to deal with the reasons for the second strike, but before I do that I'd like to ask you about various other grievances among the Asian women. Particularly, I'm thinking about the overlookers.

CHAIR. Mrs Watts, what are overlookers?

WATTS. Overlookers are in charge of shifts. They perform some skilled maintenance work and act in a general foremanly capacity.

CHAIR. I see. I'm sorry, Mrs Bhandari. You were about to tell us about your grievances.

BHANDARI. Well, there were a number of things. Attitudes. The Asian women felt, for example, that the overlookers tended to come to their machines last when they broke down, that sort of thing. And there was rudeness about lengths of tea-breaks. Small things.

WATTS. Wasn't there also something to do with toiletry arrangements?

BHANDARI. There were some problems, yes.

WATTS. Could you explain that?

BHANDARI. Well . . . sometimes the overlookers were difficult about ladies and their calls of nature.

WATTS. I'm sorry to press, but could you give an example?

BHANDARI. There was one occasion when one of the Pakistani girls was using the toilet and something had gone wrong with a loom, and the overlooker went and banged on the door and said what are you doing. So the lady replied, go home and ask your wife what she does in the toilet. Little things like that.

CHAIR. I must intervene here, Mrs Watts, because Mrs Bhandari is being, if I may say so, almost icily calm and reasonable about all this. But, as everyone knows, feeling among the Asian women was very high, and I feel that calling these matters 'little things' is something of a euphemism.

BHANDARI. Euphemism?

CHAIR. I can't immediately think of another word. Perhaps Mr Lateef –

LATEEF. I'm afraid I don't speak Gujerati, Madam Chairman.

CHAIR. Oh, of course, I apologise. I shall have to rephrase.

WATTS. Perhaps you're asking, Madam Chairman, if these matters were as trivial as Mrs Bhandari seems to indicate, why did the Asian woman take them so seriously?

CHAIR. I could not have put it better myself. We shall now let Mrs Bhandari answer the question.

BHANDARI. I think the answer is that these things add up. I think Asian women like to look up to their elders. It is traditional. They give respect to people in authority, and they expect respect to be returned. When it is not, by the overlookers, they don't understand. They get upset and then they get angry.

CHAIR. I have heard rumours that you yourself get quite angry, Mrs Bhandari. I have heard lurid tales about umbrellas on picket lines.

WATTS. I should now like to ask, Mrs Bhandari, about the situation on the 28th of May, when the strikers returned to work. I'm referring to the time-weaver position.

BHANDARI. Oh, yes. Well, as Mr Hussein said, we had thought the agreement meant that time-weavers would be selected from everybody. When we got back, we found two new time-weavers on the Dobcross day-shift. White.

CHAIR. I am going to ask Mr Clifford how the vacancies came about.

CLIFFORD. I am afraid I am not quite sure. I could take –

JOWETT. I can answer that one. One man left for a job elsewhere in the industry, for rather better pay, I gather, and the other had a heart attack and was advised to take early retirement.

CHAIR. Thank you. The point was, presumably, that the strikers felt the vacancies should not have been filled while the strike was on.

WATTS. Yes. This undermined their faith in the agreement generally.

CHAIR. And Mrs Bhandari felt that there were Asians who were as or more experienced than the people who were appointed?

BHANDARI. Yes. Not me, of course. But a couple of Asian girls and of course the Asian men on nights, a lot had worked for many years.

CHAIR. Yet, I suppose as most of the dayshift was white, there could be a language problem?

BHANDARI. Well, it was said. But, a time-weavers job is to look after machines. It is true that Dobcross looms speak neither Urdu nor Gujerati. Nor do they speak English.

WATTS. Madam Chairman, my last witness is Hameed Faruqi, who is the nightshift shop steward. Unlike a weaving loom, Mr Faruqi speaks fairly good English, but feels he would be at a disadvantage, so I would like to take his evidence through the interpreter.

CHAIR. I am quite content with that, but I would like to hear Mr Faruqi's evidence after a short adjournment.

Blackout.

Scene Four

Canteen.
   Two tables. At one, WATTS, FARUQI, BHANDARI *and* LATEEF. KITCHEN *at the other.*
   Enter JOWETT *to* KITCHEN. *He has two coffees.*

JOWETT (*sitting*). So, how's it look out front?

KITCHEN. Oh, smashing show.

JOWETT. Ay, well, you've had your entertainment. I want you up with me from now on, round that table. Might be needed.

KITCHEN. D'you know where Joan is?

JOWETT. No.

KITCHEN. She said she'd be along.

JOWETT. Ay, well, the longer out of it the better, with Mrs Dawson, in my opinion.

KITCHEN. What d'you –

   JOWETT *hushes* KITCHEN, *having noticed* WATTS *and the strikers coming past.* JOWETT *stands.*

JOWETT. Well, hallo, Mrs Watts.

WATTS. Mr Jowett.

JOWETT. And what do you think of it so far?

WATTS. Well, I can't come back with the usual reply to that, Mr Jowett. We haven't had your evidence yet.

JOWETT. I like it, Mrs Watts. You met Frank Kitchen?

WATTS. No, I haven't. How are you?

KITCHEN. Fine. Yourself?

WATTS. Oh. Wonderful.

JOWETT. I must say, Mrs B, enjoyed your crack about machines not speaking English.

BHANDARI *a slight shrug.*

WATTS. I think, conversely, we enjoyed your crack about de-womaning.

JOWETT. Oh, now, Mrs Watts, can't fault me there. I'm one hundred percent on women's lib. After all, without it, not be up against a charming lady like yourself. It's such a pleasant change.

WATTS. Ah, well, Mr Jowett, it's even worse than lady lawyers now, you know. Next year, there's equal pay.

JOWETT. Well, glory be. All this and Maggie Thatcher too. Well, I'll see you back there, Mrs Watts.

He drains his coffee, exit. KITCHEN *follows.*

WATTS. I think our Mr Jowett's what they call a trouper.

FARUQI. Pardon?

WATTS. Trouper, entertainer, joker, you know –

LATEEF *says a word to* FARUQI *in Urdu.*

FARUQI. Oh yes, very true. He likes a joke.

WATTS. Though I rather fear, it's not the trouper but his troops we need to be concerned with. Mr Kitchen.

FARUQI. Oh, no, Mr Kitchen, he's OK. Comparative.

WATTS. Comparative to what?

BHANDARI. You have not yet aquaintance with our Mrs Dawson, Mrs Watts.

WATTS *looks at* BHANDARI. *Blackout.*

Scene Five

The Court.

CHAIR, WATTS, BHANDARI, LATEEF, FARUQI, JOWETT.

WATTS. So, Mr Faruqi. You had come out on strike again, because of the appointment of the white time-weavers. You had been sacked by the company and on the 16th of June your strike had been made official. And then, two days later, the white workers voted for a new transfer scheme that had been presented to them by management, a scheme that would probably mean that a number of strikers would not be re-employed at the mill. What was your reaction to this decision?

LATEEF *translates the question to* FARUQI, *who replies in Urdu to* LATEEF. *Note:* FARUQI's *English is good enough not to need a full translation of every question, indeed, sometimes, he gives his Urdu reply without any translation.*

LATEEF. He says that the strikers felt very bad about this. They felt it was evidence of racial prejudice. The white workers were not interested in the victimization of the strikers.

WATTS. In short, the strikers felt betrayed by their fellow trade unionists?

Translation. Some chatter and laughter.

CHAIR. Yes? What is the answer?

LATEEF. The phrase is untranslatable, I'm afraid, Madam Chairman. The nearest I can get is 'To put it mildly'.

WATTS. Finally, Mr Faruqi, we have taken your evidence through an interpreter, and I think it might be asked if you have made any attempts to learn English.

LATEEF. He says he did take some lessons in Pakistan, and tried to continue them in England, but he was unable to do so.

WATTS. Whyever not?

LATEEF. Because he found it impossible to take lessons while working permanent nights with compulsory overtime.

WATTS. Thank you. That, Madam Chairman, is the case for the strike committee. But I should say that other members of the strike committee are available and can be called on later if the need arises.

CHAIR. Thank you, Mrs Watts, they are here if we need them. I have, however, just one further question for Mr Faruqi. It's a matter that has not yet arisen, but we can deal with it now. Mr Faruqi, I believe that before the strike began, you made a complaint to the Race Relations Board about the position of the night-shift workers?

FARUQI. Yes, I did.

CHAIR. When did the Board report?

FARUQI. 17th of June.

CHAIR. That was two days before the non-strikers accepted the transfer deal, which Mr Faruqi considered was evidence of racial prejudice?

FARUQI. Yes.

CHAIR. What did the Board conclude?

LATEEF. They said that no discrimination had taken place.

CHAIR. I'm sorry, you said *no* discrimination?

FARUQI. Yes.

WATTS. The strikers dispute that judgement, Madam Chairman.

CHAIR. I'm sure they do. Nonetheless, that was the Board's decision.

WATTS. Yes, it was.

CHAIR. Thank you, Mr Faruqi. I now ask Mr Jowett to put the case of the National Union of Weavers.

Lights change.

Scene Six

The Court.

CHAIR, JOWETT, KITCHEN.

JOWETT. Madam Chairman, I'd like to start by saying this. I am the General Secretary of the National Union of Weavers. Now this organisation possesses a rule-book. This in fact is it. It has 28 tightly-printed pages, and the purpose of each one of them is to keep the 9,000 members of the union as far as possible from each other's throats.

The second thing I want to point out is that there is also an agreement with the employers as to procedure on grievances. This again is it. It has a mere 18 closely-typed pages on the last of which is my signature. And that wouldn't be there if I hadn't intended to stick with it. And I am employed by my union to implement this and if I don't I am liable to lose my job.

Throughout this case I and my colleagues have been trying to resolve the contents of these two documents with the demands of the strikers at Darley Park Mill.

Now I should like to run through the events. First of all, there's the allegation that the union ignored the problems of the night-shift, until, as one of their leaders put it, the problem leapt up and bit us. Now Mr Kitchen, the senior steward, is here and can speak for himself. But all I'd say is that at the time we were moving into highly complex negotiations on the Sultzer transfer, and most of the stewards' time was taken up with that. But once we got on to it we did draw up a case, we did present it, and all of this – like writing to me and so on – flew in the face of procedure, but we did it.

Now, the actual grievances that were presented. I would like to make it plain, after Mr Hussein's evidence, that the union's view was that this was a dispute about the nightshift bonus. These other matters, promotion and the overlookers and so on, were not part of the case we presented, and this was clear in our submission to management, a copy of which went to Mr Faruqi. Now we might very well have presented these matters to management, had they been put to us before the strike began. And we did indeed talk about promotion when this appeared on the strikers' list of demands during the first strike. But it was not part of their original case, and I make that point because it explains why we were surprised when the strike began that other people, dayshift people and non-weavers came out as well. Another confusion concerns whether strike notice was given, after management rejected the claim. The strikers say I advised them not to strike, and this is right. I did that, because strike notice had not been given because it's against the rules of our union to give such notice without an executive decision. It was made plain in a letter to management and personally clear by Mr Kitchen.

Now it's in that context that subsequent events should be viewed. I've said that various horses, followed by carts, had been driven through procedure. But, notwithstanding, we negotiated for the strikers during the first strike. When they came out again, we didn't wash our hands, we tried to help and when management sacked them we made the stoppage official. And, then, when management presented the new scheme for phasing out the Dobcrosses, we advised the workforce not to take a decision till the strike was over. Now, we didn't persuade them, but we tried.

CHAIR. Forgive me, Mr Jowett, but I think it's worth asking, what were the new proposals?

KITCHEN. If I could –

CHAIR. Certainly, Mr Kitchen.

KITCHEN. They weren't, I mean, they weren't quite the same as the ones we'd rejected in 1973. There was a new item in the package, which was that a few dayshift jobs'd be preserved, on Dobcrosses, for special, short-run work. It's happened elsewhere in the industry.

CHAIR. However, there still had to be some compulsory redundancies?

KITCHEN. Yuh.

CHAIR. What was the voting on the package?

KITCHEN. Virtually unanimous.

CHAIR. Despite what Mr Jowett said.

KITCHEN. Despite what Mr Jowett said.

JOWETT. I think, to intervene myself, the workers felt that with the grant-aid money running out, and, frankly with the industry in a dip again, I think they felt they'd played out all the rope.

CHAIR. I see.

JOWETT. That's really it, except to say, we think we've proved that the question isn't why we didn't push hard enough, but the reason why we pushed so hard. And the reason was, we felt that here we had a group of people, most new to the industry, they didn't all speak English, and they had a grievance, so we said, OK, we'll bend the rules a bit, and we did. That's all.

CHAIR. Thank you. We will now break for lunch.

Blackout.

Scene Seven

Canteen.

DAWSON *sits reading a magazine and eating an apple.* FARUQI *and* BHANDARI *cross the stage. She watches them pass. Enter* JOWETT.

JOWETT. Well, hallo, Mrs D.

DAWSON. Hallo, George.

JOWETT. Mite delayed, eh?

DAWSON. Ay. A bit of upset.

DAWSON *pats her stomach. She's pregnant.*

JOWETT. All right now?

DAWSON. They say the little bastard's shifting to the left.

JOWETT. I'm saying nothing.

DAWSON. So, what's she like?

JOWETT. The Baroness? Oh, think she's what you'd call, well-meaning soul. A coffee-morning type, you know. The sort donates her mink to Oxfam.

DAWSON. Well, George, see our case doesn't go the same road, eh?

JOWETT. Oh, don't you worry, Joan. It's in safe hands. We'll win.

DAWSON. Ay, well, that all depends, dunnit.

JOWETT. All depends on what?

DAWSON. On who you mean by 'we'.

JOWETT. We is our members, Joan. We is the union. (*Looks at his watch.*) Well, better go.

DAWSON (*stands*). OK, what happens now?

JOWETT. Well, now I've done my case, it's them.

DAWSON. Who's them?

JOWETT. Them's who them always is. Them is the employers. Joan.

Blackout.

Scene Eight

The Court.

CHAIR, CLIFFORD.

CLIFFORD. Madam Chairman, there have been a number of allegations flying about to the effect that the company has been tardy or laggardly in its attempts to reach a settlement of this dispute.

Madam Chairman, like all other weaving companies, Darley Park has contractual arrangements with clothing manufacturers who in their turn have commitments to the wholesale and retail clothing trades. At the other end of the operation, the firm is committed to spinning mills who have arrangements with carding and combing concerns who have contracts with raw material suppliers.

In short, we are in the middle of a long process of getting wool off the back of sheep and on to the backs of people in the shortest possible time, and any part of that process which disrupts the smooth running of the whole will quickly lose its confidence.

Now, having said that, Madam Chairman, I would like to move on to the Sultzer transfer. Madam, Darley Park Mills has a number of responsibilities, but it believes that its over-riding duty is to stay in existence, to continue to provide employment for its workers, a service to its customers and dividends to its shareholders.

CHAIR. I trust the company's priorities are in that order and not the reverse.

CLIFFORD. I think the company would view all three as mutually dependent, Madam Chairman.

CHAIR. I am not convinced that everyone here would agree with that, Mr Clifford, but do go on.

CLIFFORD. Thank you. The point I was making was that the company has determined that the only way for it to remain competitive is to complete the transfer, and it's in that context that I'd like you to consider the management's actions. First of all, there is the claim presented by Mr Jowett on the 5th of May.

Now, despite some controversy about what was being claimed, it is agreed that the main demand was on the night-shift bonus on the Dobcrosses, and I'm sure it's obvious that the management had to turn it down, precisely because it would have had the effect of delaying the phasing out of the Dobcross looms. Now, the next –

CHAIR. I'm sorry, Mr Clifford . . . Are you saying that the company refused to improve the conditions of the Dobcross workers in order to encourage them to accept the phasing out?

CLIFFORD. That's more or less right, Madam Chairman. I'm sure you understand their point of view.

CHAIR. It's certainly understandable, Mr Clifford. It also sounds to me like blackmail.

CLIFFORD. I'm sure the company would not accept that word.

CHAIR. Can it think of an alternative?

CLIFFORD. I think it would prefer the word 'incentive'.

CHAIR. Yes. I see.

CLIFFORD. This desire to conclude the transfer speedily was also the reason why the company accepted what has been called the Ridley Agreement, which did propose a small increase in the nightshift bonus, but in the context of a commitment by all sides to a rapid recommencement of the phasing out, in the interests not only of the company, but also those of racial harmony.

Now the company has been criticised for pressing ahead with its new scheme during the second strike. There are really two points here. The first is that the company, despite the fact that the strikers had demonstrably broken their contracts of employment, stayed its hand a week before issuing termination notices, in the hope that wiser counsels would prevail.

But, and this is the second point, there was no question that whether or not the strikers returned, the Scheme would have to be implemented. Negotiations were already in progress. They then received Mrs Ridley's blessing. I think you will understand that the company, who had advocated this scheme for so long, had no choice but to seize with both hands the chance of implementing it.

Finally, Madam Chairman, I would like to state quite unequivocally that there is no question in the company's mind of any distinction between its employees on the grounds of race, colour, creed or national origin. It would be foolish to deny, however, that there are those within the mill for whom this is a question. The company has not in any way given into these pressures, but has tried, by a process of gradual persuasion, to allay what it regards as groundless fears.

That is all I want to say for the moment, Madam Chairman. I should say that Mr Eric Harper, the Managing Director, is here if there are any questions that go beyond my brief.

Lights change.

Scene Nine

The Court.

CHAIR, CLIFFORD, HARPER, WATTS, LATEEF, FARUQI.

CHAIR. Ladies and gentlemen, having concluded the initial statements, we now enter a general questioning session. As Mr Clifford's case is fresh in our minds, it would be best to start with him and/or Mr Harper. My first question concerns the whole question of the new two time-weavers, over which, if I may say so, Mr Clifford managed somewhat to slide. Now, perhaps Mr Harper could help us here. These two vacancies, first, one was someone who'd left the firm, the other had suffered a coronary, is that right?

HARPER. Yes.

CHAIR. And how were the replacements selected?

HARPER. They were selected from a list of people who applied when we posted the vacancies. I should point out that none of the applicants was an Asian. They were appointed in accordance with our normal procedures, procedures that everyone had been perfectly happy with until –

CHAIR. I beg your pardon, Mr Harper, but Mrs Watts is making semaphore signals at me. I haven't been in the navy, but I think she means 'stop'.

WATTS. Madam Chairman, with respect, it is hardly surprising no Asians applied, as most of them were on strike at the time.

HARPER. With respect, that was not a situation of the company's choosing.

WATTS. Well, with great respect, it is possible to argue that the company might have waited until the strike was over and the Asians were back at work before filling the vacancies.

HARPER. Well, with the greatest respect, it was not the company's fault that most of the dayshift was still working. Had they *all* been on strike, there would have been no need to fill the vacancies. As it was –

WATTS. With the greatest of all possible respect, Mr Harper –

CHAIR. Mrs Watts, and Mr Harper, I may not be alone in thinking that if we have much more respect in this Inquiry, mutual or otherwise, we shall suffocate.

WATTS. I'm so sorry, Madam Chairman.

CHAIR (*smiling*). There really is no need. I was merely . . .

LATEEF. Um, I think Mr Faruqi has a point here.

CHAIR. Yes?

A little translation.

LATEEF. He is wondering if management seriously argues that the vacancies that occurred were as they say coincidence.

CHAIR. I am sure that Mr Faruqi is not suggesting that a heart attack is anything but coincidence.

I think we had better leave that there. I wish now to ask the company about the sacking of the strikers in the second stoppage. Mr Clifford, do you or Mr Harper wish to deal with this?

CLIFFORD. I can deal with this, Madam Chairman; it's a matter on which my brief is quite comprehensive.

Lights change.

Scene Ten

The Court.

CHAIR, WATTS, LATEEF, FARUQI, BHANDARI, CLIFFORD.

CLIFFORD. Madam Chairman, the company's argument on this has nothing to do with whether strike notice was or wasn't given and at what stage. The point is that, in law, workers are employed to work and if they do not do so, if for example they simply decide to stay away, they are in breach of their contracts of employment. There is no contractual right to give notice of an intention to stop work, and then to say, 'We have stopped work, but we have not broken our contracts because we told you we were going to do it seven days ago'.

CHAIR. Are you saying that any strike is a breach of contract of employment?

CLIFFORD. I am saying that unless there are specific agreements that is the case. There are agreements between employers and trade unions which say something like 'there shall be so many days' strike notice', in which case it's possible to say that a bona fide stoppage of work is provided for. There is, however, no such clause in any agreement that I can locate between the employers' organisations and the National Union of Weavers.

CHAIR. But surely, Mr Clifford, there must be custom and practice on this.

CLIFFORD. Indeed there could be, Madam Chairman. But in this case there is none because this is the first official strike organised by the N.U.W. in the last 40 years.

BHANDARI *laughs.* LATEEF *whispers to* FARUQI. FARUQI *laughs.*

CHAIR. Um, I would point out to the Strike Committee, Mrs Watts, that having a strike-free record is not necessarily a matter for scorn.

WATTS. Well, I'm sure they take your point. It could be argued however that this strike demonstrated that the union's procedures are inadequate.

CHAIR. It could be argued, Mrs Watts, that the best test of a country's defences is a war, but it's not necessarily the best excuse for waging one.

CLIFFORD. Madam, the only thing I'd say on this is that it could be asked, under these circumstances, why the company delayed as long as it did before terminating the strikers' contracts.

CHAIR. Yes, I suppose it could be asked.

CLIFFORD. The answer, Madam Chairman, is that the company was then, as it has always been, throughout this dispute, giving every benefit of every doubt, and bending over backwards to be fair.

Lights change.

Scene Eleven

CHAIR, WATTS, JOWETT, FARUQI, LATEEF, BHANDARI, DAWSON.

CHAIR. The next question I want to ask concerns the strike Committee, but I think it would be useful before that to establish one or two things about the union organisation and the grievance procedure. Mr Jowett, I'm sure you'll want to comment on what Mr Clifford has just said, but I wonder if you could circumvent the right-to-strike question at this moment?

JOWETT. Well, yes, Madam Chairman, I'm glad of that, because it's something on which I would have waxed somewhat lyrical, at some length and in some passion, and my doctor would protest most strongly at the likely effects on my blood pressure.

CHAIR. Heaven forbid, Mr Jowett. Perhaps you could begin by outlining the union structure at the mill.

JOWETT. Well, the basic unit is the factory committee, which consists of shop stewards from each section, including warp-preparation, mending, and so on. In weaving, there are four stewards, one for Dobcross nights, one for days, and two for the Sultzers.

CHAIR. I dislike these questions, but could you tell me the racial breakdown of the stewards at the moment?

JOWETT. Well, there's nothing sinister about this, they reflect the composition of the sheds. The two Sultzer stewards are English, Mr Faruqi represents the nightshift, and the dayshift is looked after by Mrs Dawson, who is also with us, and seems to be a light pinkish colour.

CHAIR. Can I ask, as Mr Faruqi is on permanent nights, if there are any problems about attending meetings and so on?

JOWETT. Well, yes, there are obvious problems there, unfortunately.

CHAIR. Peculiarly so, I would have thought, under the circumstances. And the grievance procedure?

JOWETT. Well, I won't go through it all, but the first step is for a person to see the shop steward and then go with him to the senior overlooker in the shed.

CHAIR. Yes. Of course, in this case, the shop steward is 'her', and I would like to ask Mrs Dawson a question or two.

JOWETT. Please go ahead.

CHAIR. Mrs Dawson, were you aware that there was discontent among the Asian women on the Dobcross dayshift?

DAWSON. Well, I think I overhead things, ay.

CHAIR. Did you receive any official complaint?

DAWSON. No, I didn't.

CHAIR. When the Asian women came out on strike, did they talk to you about it at all?

DAWSON. They did not. They had a meeting, with their nightshift people, and next thing I knew, they was all on a picket line.

CHAIR. So really, it would be fair to say that neither the union procedure nor the grievance procedure had been followed correctly.

DAWSON. No, I'd disagree with that.

CHAIR. You would?

DAWSON. It weren't a matter, procedure not followed correctly. It were a matter, procedure not followed at all.

CHAIR. Thank you. Can I ask Mrs Bhandari if Mrs Dawson is correct in saying that no complaints were presented to her?

BHANDARI. I do not recall if any were.

CHAIR. You mean, a far as you recall, they weren't?

BHANDARI. Yes.

CHAIR. Second, can I ask who told you or asked you to come out on strike?

BHANDARI. We were asked by the nightshift men at a meeting.

CHAIR. Third, did you at any time, before the meeting or after it, ask Mrs Dawson her opinion or consult her in any way?

BHANDARI. We did not consult her in any way.

CHAIR. In any way at all?

BHANDARI. In any way at all.

WATTS. I think, Madam Chairman, that there is behind this a whole legacy, which I would like with your permission to deal with as a piece as it were –

CHAIR. Well, I'm sure you will deal with it, Mrs Watts, but before you do so I would like to clear up one further matter. Can I ask Mr Faruqi. Did he in fact think that the union had given strike notice?

LATEEF. He says that the workers made it clear what they wished the union to do.

CHAIR. Yes, but having made it clear, did he think the union responded to their wishes?

LATEEF. He says that the management had refused to give in to the demands.

CHAIR. Well, again that's not the question I asked. Whatever the workers thought, does he think that the union in fact gave notice to strike?

LATEEF. He says yes.

CHAIR. That is what I wanted to establish because I have read Mr
   Jowett's letter to management and I must point out that it seems
   quite clear that strike notice was *not* given.

   WATTS *finds letter.* FARUQI *finds another copy in his pocket.* LATEEF
   looks over FARUQI's *shoulder.*

   I quote: 'We have advised the workers against industrial action,
   but I must inform you that feeling is so strong that they have
   pressed us to give you seven days' strike notice'.
   Now, that must mean, despite the Asians' feelings, that the
   union did not –

LATEEF (*looking at the letter*). Oh, no.

CHAIR. Mr Lateef?

LATEEF. Oh, no, it mustn't mean that.

CHAIR. I'm sorry?

LATEEF. I mean, it needn't mean that. It's ambiguous. I mean, it
   could mean something else.

WATTS. Madam, can I consult a moment?

CHAIR. Yes, I think perhaps you should.

   Lights change.

Scene Twelve

The Court.
   CHAIR, WATTS, JOWETT, DAWSON, KITCHEN.

WATTS. Madam Chairman, you quoted the relevant passage of the
   letter of the 8th of May, and pointed out that it could be
   interpreted as meaning that strike notice was not given.

CHAIR. Yes?

WATTS. Now, what Mr Lateef noticed, which I must confess I
   hadn't spotted, was that that sentence could mean two opposite
   things.

CHAIR. Go on.

WATTS. It could of course mean, as you said, that the phrase 'they
   have pressed us to give strike notice' is presented merely as
   evidence for the strong feelings among the Asians, and, indeed,

there is the phrase 'we have advised the workers against industrial action' to confirm that view. However, I maintain that it could also mean that, despite the union's advice, the workers were insisting on industrial action, and the phrase 'they have pressed us to give strike notice' means 'we are giving strike notice, and this is it'.

JOWETT. Madam Chairman, of course the former view is the correct one, we were telling management that we were under pressure, and frankly, I think this could be a case, this isn't a racial point, but as we know some of the people don't have perfect English –

CHAIR. Mr Jowett, I must interrupt you. It is Mrs Watts who finds the letter ambiguous, and her command of English appears to be exemplary. Also, I hope I'm reasonably fluent in the language, and I must confess that now I look at it, it seems ambiguous to me.

JOWETT. Well, all right then, forgetting that I can't speak English –

CHAIR. Come now, Mr Jowett, you speak it splendidly. I've heard it whispered it's your mother tongue.

JOWETT. You haven't met my mother, Madam Chairman.

CHAIR. I'm sure it would be a pleasure and a privilege.

KITCHEN. Look, I'm sorry, Madam Chairman, but whatever's in the letter, I did make the position clear to a member of the strike committee, on the 8th of May.

CHAIR. Who was that?

KITCHEN. It was Abdul Kadir.

CHAIR. I'm sorry, who is –

JOWETT. Abdul Kadir worked in the warehouse, Madam Chairman. He was not a permanent worker, in fact, but a student. He was one of the main spokesmen for the strike committee.

CHAIR. Mrs Watts, is Mr Kadir here?

WATTS. Madam Chairman, I'm afraid that Abdul Kadir isn't here.

CHAIR. But is it possible to –

WATTS. He's unable to attend the hearing, I'm afraid.

CHAIR. Well, I suppose we must accept that.

WATTS. Nonetheless, and whatever meetings may have taken place, it is quite clear the letter is ambiguous.

CHAIR. I think we can agree, the only thing that is clear is the manifest unclearness of that letter.

DAWSON. Madam, can I make a point?

CHAIR. Yes, of course.

DAWSON. It does seem blind obvious.

CHAIR. I'm sure we'd all welcome a blind obvious point.

DAWSON. Surely it's obvious that if these people knew procedure, they'd have known that Mr Kitchen, even Mr Jowett, couldn't give strike notice without going to the union executive. I mean, that's lesson one.

CHAIR. Well, I take that point, but we have already established that for various reasons the Asians were not fully aware of procedure.

DAWSON. Ay, well, a person might not know there's a law against murder, but don't stop him going to prison if he kills someone.

CHAIR. Well, I'm not convinced that that's a very helpful analogy –

JOWETT. Madam Chairman, can I come in. I think the point Mrs Dawson's making is that if the letter can be taken in two ways, then knowing what the rules are and all other things being equal, the strikers couldn't –

WATTS. Can I point out to Mr Jowett, that if all other things were equal, then we wouldn't be here.

A pause before lights change.

Scene Thirteen

The Court.

CHAIR, WATTS, DAWSON, BHANDARI, SANDHU, HUSSEIN, JOWETT, KITCHEN.

WATTS. Madam Chairman, a few moments ago, it was revealed that the strikers had not followed correct union procedure. With your permission, I would like to probe the reasons for that a little with Mrs Bhandari.

CHAIR. Certainly.

WATTS. Mrs Bhandari, you said earlier that you didn't trust Mrs Dawson and, by implication, the union. I'd like to try to discover why. First, are you a member of the National Union of Weavers?

BHANDARI. Yes.

WATTS. Did you join immediately you started work at the mill?

BHANDARI. No, it was about a month later.

WATTS. Who invited you to join?

BHANDARI. Mr Hussein.

WATTS. Who is not on your shift, and indeed is not a shop steward?

BHANDARI. No.

WATTS. And had you been approached at all by Mrs Dawson or any other shop steward?

BHANDARI. No, I had not.

WATTS. Now, I believe elections for shop steward take place in March. Am I right in thinking you decided to stand for election this year?

BHANDARI. Yes, I did.

WATTS. Now we know you didn't win, because Mrs Dawson is still your shop steward. But how well did you do?

BHANDARI. I didn't.

CHAIR. Sorry, you mean you didn't do well?

BHANDARI. I didn't do at all. I was not allowed to stand.

WATTS. What reason was given for that?

BHANDARI. Because I had not been a member of the union for two years. Apparently there is a rule.

JOWETT. Madam Chairman –

WATTS. I would be grateful if I could finish with Mrs Bhandari before Mr Jowett comments.

CHAIR. Would you mind, Mr Jowett?

JOWETT. Not at all.

WATTS. Now can I ask why you feel people did not make use of the grievance procedure.

BHANDARI. Well, part of the problem is that you go first to the senior overlooker, and a lot of the girls don't want to do that.

WATTS. Why not?

BHANDARI. Because it was mostly him they had a complaint about.

WATTS. Yes. Is there any other reason?

BHANDARI. Well, it's hard to say. But, let me . . . Say you have a little grievance. And you don't, it seems so silly, make a fuss. And then your friend, she has another silly grievance. And her friend another. And together, they stop looking so silly. But, of course, you cannot put them together.

WATTS. So what you're saying is that the procedure can't by its nature cope with grievances that are as it were cumulative and collective. That a worker is not going to nit-pick over a small thing, which on its own looks trivial, but which taken together with other things add up to evidence of something else.

CHAIR. Perhaps Mrs Bhandari could hazard what that something else might be.

BHANDARI. I suppose, that someone, somewhere, is prejudiced against you.

WATTS. Thank you, that's all.

CHAIR. Mr Jowett?

JOWETT. Well, all I want to say is that there is indeed a rule that elected people have to be financial members of the union for two years. But that applies to everyone.

WATTS. But I'm sure Mr Jowett would agree that in effect –

JOWETT. This rule was adopted in October 1953.

WATTS. Look, no-one's suggesting that this rule was *intended* to discriminate –

JOWETT. Well, thanks –

WATTS. – but it's my argument that in the context of all the other factors that is the effect of that rule. Madam Chairman, I would like to discuss a couple of those factors with Mr Ranjit Singh Sandhu, who works in the Sultzer shed.

CHAIR. This is still your reply to the union?

WATTS. Yes, it is.

CHAIR. Then, very well.

WATTS. Mr Sandhu, how long have you worked at Darley Park?

SANDHU. From leaving school. Seven years.

WATTS. And because of that relatively long experience, you were moved to the Sultzers two years ago.

SANDHU. That's right.

WATTS. And it's also fair to say that you're good at your job?

SANDHU. Well, I suppose . . . I used to earn good piecework. I think I'm good at it.

WATTS. And in the normal run of events, you'd expect to get promotion, I mean, you might see yourself becoming a time-weaver?

CHAIR. Not now, surely, Mrs Watts? Mr Sandhu is only 22.

WATTS. No, I'm not suggesting that. Mr Sandhu, do you think you will become a time-weaver at some stage?
SANDHU. I very much doubt it.

WATTS. Why not?

SANDHU. I think promotion for Asians became a dead duck two years ago.

WATTS. Why then?

SANDHU. Because it was then that a white was put in as a time-weaver on the nightshift.

CHAIR. We have had this before. Wasn't an Asian subsequently appointed as well?

WATTS. Yes, but what I wanted to ask Mr Sandhu was what the reaction of the white workers on the Sultzers was to this incident.

SANDHU. They were, one could say, not too chirpy.

WATTS. But couldn't you see the point? They were worried that the man who had been appointed might be demoted to make way for the Asian.

SANDHU. But he wasn't demoted.

WATTS. Yes, but I was suggesting –

SANDHU. And still, that was not what bothered them.

WATTS. What did bother them?

SANDHU. What bothered them was the Asian being promoted.

WATTS. I see. And it was the memory of this incident, and the white workers' attitudes, it was because of this that you were so concerned when, in this dispute, you came back off strike and found the two new time-weavers on the dayshift?

SANDHU. I think that's called a rhetorical question.

CHAIR. Could you answer it nonetheless.

SANDHU. Of course we were, as you say, concerned.

WATTS. Finally, there has been criticism of people not concerned with the dispute, coming out on strike. You work on the Sultzers. Why did you join the strike?

SANDHU. The question is the other way round. Why did the whites not come out with us. Why, even when it was made official, did the union allow them to keep working. That's the question you should ask.

WATTS. All right. Will you answer it?

SANDHU. The whites did not come out because they are so racialist that they are prepared to destroy their union rather than let us get promotion. You asked why I came out. I came out when my people came and asked me to.

JOWETT. Right. I'm going to answer that. I'm actually quite pleased that Mr Sandhu's said what he has said. I'm pleased because at last you're hearing the real voice of this dispute. What's actually been happening. The kind of things, been hearing on the picket line. You mentioned Mrs Bhandari seeming calm and cool. You haven't, with respect, been through a picket-line and had her shriek abuse at you.

CHAIR. When you say abuse?

JOWETT. Well, I don't know, Madam Chairman. One thing they shout's a word that sounds like cha-cha. Don't know it, it's s'posed to be a joke about the way I walk –

WATTS. The word is chancha, I'm informed. Roughly translated, it means a lackey of the management.

JOWETT. Oh, well, I thought it might be on those lines. And I think if we're flinging words like lackey and racialist around, then we might as well say some other things, and admit for starters that for all this talk about machines not speaking English, there are language problems and experience problems and they're not the only problems that face us and we'd best be straight on that and all.

CHAIR. Go on.

JOWETT. Well. It's just – a fact. There are fears. P'raps I don't quite share them. But I'm not going to deny them.

CHAIR. What do you mean?

JOWETT. I mean, there's fears, among the English workers, that in three years time, won't be a white face left.

SANDHU. Oh, yes, now he –

JOWETT (*Mostly at* SANDHU *now*), Cos there's people there who've worked their lives –

CHAIR. Mr Jowett –

JOWETT. And it wouldn't matter if you were all Germans, Japanese or Buddhist monks –

CHAIR. Mr Jowett, I'm afraid you can't have it both ways. You implied a moment ago that the Asian workers are incapable of doing the job, and that could be true. You've just said they might be so good that they'll take over the mill, and that could be true as well. But they can't both be true, and I'd suggest in fact that neither –

JOWETT. All I'm saying is you've got to understand –

SANDHU. All you're saying is, you won't support your –

JOWETT. Look, you, we've bent over backwards, and I know that you're not used to how we –

SANDHU. Not used? Not used to being used as slaves!

DAWSON *laughs loudly*.

CHAIR. What's funny, Mrs Dawson?

DAWSON. Oh, dear me. Oh just you hear him. We're not used to being slaves. We're not like British workers, not prepared to graft all hours for lousy wages. We are proud and dignified.

CHAIR. I'm not quite sure . . .

DAWSON. They came. Eight year ago. They came and they did nights and they did overtime. Don't ask me, ask George Jowett. Ask how long he'd fought, get rid of people being forced to do nights overtime. And nearly won it too. And then they came, and yes sir, no sir, eight hours, ten hours, twelve hours full sir.

SANDHU. So why when we go on strike to get rid of it –

DAWSON. Oh, ay, and you'll hear all about union solidarity and black and white unite and fight and brotherhood of man. You heard him? What he said just then? It's when *my* people said come out, he came out. We are not his people.

SANDHU. No, you are not my people.

DAWSON. But when we say, we stand up for our own kind, that is racialist. When we protect our own jobs, oh, that's racialist. When we say –

SANDHU (*to* CHAIR). Now, you listen. Listen. Now you're hearing all this filth that we have had throughout this –

DAWSON (*she makes to go*). Well, I'm not stopping here to get abused, I think I'll –

CHAIR. No, you will *not* go, Mrs Dawson. You will sit down, as will Mr Sandhu.

After a pause, they sit.

Ladies and gentlemen, I had hoped that this Inquiry would serve to bring together the parties in a calm and reasonable atmosphere. I had feared, however, that if these proceedings became uncalm and irrational, then they might tend to exacerbate the tensions that gave rise to this hearing. I'm very sorry that my fears should have been so amply confirmed. It is not yet five o'clock, but I see no alternative at this time but to adjourn for the day.

WATTS. Madam Chairman. I would like to say one thing before this session closes.

CHAIR. Well, you may, Mrs Watts, but I would ask that it be brief and a great deal more temperate than the statements we have just been hearing.

WATTS. It is brief and I hope it is temperate. It's just that earlier in the day, it was claimed that there were, I think the word that Mr Clifford used was pressures, racist pressures, from the workforce, on the company. I think it should be pointed out that what Mrs Dawson and, to a certain extent, Mr Jowett have said might be seen to confirm that point of view. (*Pause.*) That's all.

Lights change.

Scene Fourteen

The Court.
> WATTS *clearing up her papers.* BHANDARI, HUSSEIN *waiting for her.*
DAWSON *stands there. The* OTHERS *have gone.*

DAWSON. Eh. Mrs Watts.

WATTS. Yes, Mrs Dawson?

DAWSON. Where d'you live?

WATTS. In London. Why?

DAWSON. Where, London?

WATTS. Highgate Village.

DAWSON. Highgate Village. Ay, well, that explains it.

WATTS. What?

DAWSON. There's plenty of them there.

WATTS. I'm sorry?

DAWSON. Just wait till one moves in next door.

> WATTS *picks up her papers to go.*

Eh, Mrs Watts. Your kids go 'way to school?

WATTS. We haven't any kids.

DAWSON. Oh, see. I have. Two. And this one on the way. You
ought to see their school.

WATTS. Why?

DAWSON. Cos more Mohammads there than there are in bloody Mecca.

Pause.

WATTS. I'm sorry, Mrs Dawson . . .

DAWSON. Eh – Not that – Not, 'sorry, Mrs Dawson' – after what
you said just now.

WATTS. What did I say just now?

DAWSON. You said it. Not me. You said you was on the bosses' side.

> DAWSON *goes out.*

WATTS (*to herself*). I didn't . . .

HUSSEIN. Um, well . . . in a way, you did.

> WATTS *looks at* HUSSEIN. WATTS *looks at* BHANDARI. *Blackout.*

Scene Fifteen

Pub.

SANDHU *and* HUSSEIN *leaning on the bar with their pints.*

HUSSEIN. How d'you think it's going?

SANDHU. Better. Better than this morning.

HUSSEIN. Yes.

SANDHU. Things coming out.

HUSSEIN. Things coming out.
    Pause.

Hey, want a game of darts?

SANDHU. I didn't know you played.

HUSSEIN. I'm in the team. Pub team.

SANDHU. I don't play darts.

    Pause. Something amuses HUSSEIN. *He smiles.*

HUSSEIN. Hey. You remember that bloke, who got arrested.
    Something Khan.

SANDHU. Haider.

HUSSEIN. Yuh. And he was up in court and the magistrate said,
    'Can you speak English', and he said 'no, no English'.

SANDHU. Mm.

HUSSEIN. Cos he'd been told by someome you did better if you
    have no English. You know, poor old bugger, speaks no
    English, being crippled, got to make allowances. And the guy
    said, 'Very well' and so has the interpreter. (HUSSEIN *is beginning
    to laugh at his own story.*) And then the magistrate said, asked, 'it
    has been established', this was what he said, 'it has been
    established that Mrs Khan was among the most forceful of the
    picket leaders. Can you enquire of Mr Khan' this was the
    question, see, 'can you inquire if Mr Khan's behaviour can be
    explained by the influence of his wife?' You remember Mrs
    Khan?

SANDHU. Indeed I remember Mrs Khan.

HUSSEIN (*laughing*). And, before the interpreter has a chance, Khan
    leaps straight in and says: 'Well, your lordship, I don't know if
    that kind of thing happens in your house, but it certainly doesn't

happen in mine'.

HUSSEIN *laughing merrily.* SANDHU *is not sure he has followed.*

You see, he said he spoke no English, and so the magistrate, of course, went quite bananas. And he got three months.

SANDHU *now sure he hasn't followed.* HUSSEIN *laughing like a drain. To explain:*

Suspended, you know.

He laughs.

'But it certainly doesn't happen in mine'.

SANDHU *taps* HUSSEIN's *arm. He's noticed that* KITCHEN *has appeared further down the bar.* HUSSEIN *stops laughing.* A BARTENDER *appears with a drink. He stands there.*

SANDHU. That Khan went back of course.

HUSSEIN (*sips his beer*). Yes, well. They did. Can understand.

HUSSEIN. They want a quiet life. Just make a little money, then go home.

SANDHU. You going home?

HUSSEIN. I s'pose I think I'm going to go home.

KITCHEN *goes over to the* ASIANS.

KITCHEN. I didn't know you drank in here.

HUSSEIN. Oh, yes. I'm in the darts team.

KITCHEN. Oh, ay?

HUSSEIN (*glances at* SANDHU). Yes. We drink in here.

KITCHEN. It's not against your faith?

HUSSEIN. Oh, I'm not a good Moslem. In fact, I'm a terrible Moslem. And Ranjit here's a Sikh, and they do anything.

Pause.

KITCHEN. Hey, thought, right funny, all that stuff, we haven't got the right to strike. George Jowett turning blue.

HUSSEIN. Oh, yes.

KITCHEN. A man of moderation, George. The quiet life.

HUSSEIN. Well, some of us, as well, quite like the quiet life.

KITCHEN. No, I meant, he's not, for me, not militant enough.

HUSSEIN. I see.

Slight pause.

KITCHEN. He better get in quick, though, with a claim, when this lot's over.

HUSSEIN. Why?

KITCHEN. Well, you know, the Common Market referendum, now we lost that, moving Tony Benn and all. I'll bet you, TUC'll cave in, and we'll have bloody wage controls.

HUSSEIN. Didn't they say they wouldn't –

KITCHEN. Oh, they always *say*.

Slight pause.

So, slap our claim in double quick.

SANDHU. Our claim.

KITCHEN. That's right.

Pause.

She is, Joan, she's a good militant. A damn sight better than George Jowett. Just, she's got a blind spot. S'all. Her uncle got shot, in Calcutta, in the Army, 1946.

SANDHU. My uncle got shot too. In Burma. 1943.

KITCHEN. Oh, ay. I know 'bout that. Sikh regiments. The best of all.

Pause.

Where d'you actually come from?

SANDHU. Me? I come from Bradford.

KITCHEN. Sorry, no I mean before that.

SANDHU. Oh for a bit I was in Leeds.

KITCHEN. Sorry, I didn't, meant, where did you come from.

SANDHU. Oh, sorry, see what you mean. Where was I *born*.

KITCHEN. That's right.

SANDHU. Southall.

Pause.

HUSSEIN. I'm from Lahore. My mother came in 1961. To be a

nurse. In answer to a Government advertisement. The Ministry of Health, they wanted people for the hospitals.

KITCHEN. Yuh, well –

HUSSEIN. The Minister at that time was a man called Right Hon Enoch Powell.

Pause.

KITCHEN. I'm not a Powellite. I don't think you should all go back.

SANDHU. Look. OK. It's very nice, you come and drink with us. We're very touched. But, really, don't tell us, you do not wish repatriation. Go and tell your Mrs Dawson.

KITCHEN. Look, I'm not –

SANDHU. Cos we are not the problem. She's the problem. And she's not our problem. She is yours.

Pause. KITCHEN *shrugs.*

KITCHEN. Play it your way.

He's about to say something else. Changes his mind, takes his pint and exits. Pause.

HUSSEIN. You know, you want to find the biggest racialists of all, you go to India and Pakistan. Oh boy.

SANDHU. I've never been to India or Pakistan. I live in England.

Long pause. HUSSEIN *starts chuckling.*

What?

HUSSEIN *chuckling.*

HUSSEIN. 'Well, your lordship . . . I don't know if that happens in your house . . .'

SANDHU *smiles.*

'But it certainly . . .'

HUSSEIN's *laughter is infectious.*

'It certainly doesn't happen in mine . . .'

HUSSEIN *laughing fit to burst.* SANDHU *picks it up. The two men laugh and laugh. Blackout.*

Scene Sixteen

DAWSON'S *house.*

DAWSON *and her* VISITOR *sitting facing each other. They are drinking tea. Pause before* DAWSON *speaks.*

DAWSON. I mean, you'd not believe the things they're saying. Think we owe them everything. That everything that's done to them's our fault. It's us to blame, that they're cheap labour.

Pause.

I mean, I know what's going to happen. Everybody knows. If they get this, then every time a job comes up, if they don't get it, it's discrimination. Three year, all be gone. Why shouldn't we stand up to stop that happening? We've got rights too.

Slight pause.

D'you want another cup?

The VISITOR *shakes her head.*

OK.

Slight pause.

See, take a place like this. And what it used to be. It's all gone rusty. Not just them. The state of things. The shops all full of mucky magazines. The whole thing tarnished. Mouldy.

Pause.

We know what happens. Area like this. I mean, it's just the facts of life. They come in, and a place just drops apart. It's just a fact of life.

Slight pause.

Dunno where John is.

Slight smile.

Never do.

VISITOR *smiles sympathetically.*

I sometimes feel split off. Detached from things around. All look the same. Same streets, and full of people. But it's like you're in a perspex box. Can see, but reach out, you can't touch them. Don't know who you are.

Pause.

Why should I? Feel guilty? They're the ones as should feel guilty. What they done to us. To me. It's not me should feel guilty.

Slight pause.

Got a cigarette?

The VISITOR *shakes her head.*

Good. I shouldn't, really, now.

Slight pause.

I mean, I don't, don't blame them. Personally. Think they're just as much the victims. Blame the people let them in and blame the people who inflame them once they're here.

Pause.

You've got to ask what is behind all this. You've got to ask *why* people let them in.

Slight pause.

I mean. How can I bring a person into this, when I don't know the reason for what's happening, and who's behind it all. What can I say?

Pause.

VISITOR. We think we've got an inkling of what's happening. And who's behind it all.

Slight pause.

DAWSON. You know –

VISITOR (*stands*). Well, look. The time.

She takes a newspaper and books from her bag.

I've got your copy of the paper. And a book or two you might have time to read.

She gives them to DAWSON.

You'll tell me what you think?

DAWSON. I will.

The VISITOR *turns to go.*

You know, before you came, I didn't . .

VISITOR *looks back.*

You know, I really didn't have, before I joined . . .

She doesn't say anything else. The VISITOR *smiles.*

VISITOR. I'll see myself out, now. Good night.

She goes. DAWSON *sits holding the books and newspaper.*

DAWSON. You see . . . I've grown up since you came.

Lights fade.

ACT TWO

Scene Seventeen

Hotel.

CLIFFORD *and* HARPER *are finishing breakfast.*

CLIFFORD *has had croissants and coffee.* HARPER *has had cooked breakfast and tea.*

CLIFFORD *offers a cigarette to* HARPER.

CLIFFORD. Cigarette?

HARPER. No thanks.

CLIFFORD *lights his cigarette.*

CLIFFORD. I'm always full of admiration, people who can eat their way through all that flesh first thing. Sure it's a sign of moral fibre.

HARPER. Well, I –

CLIFFORD. Coffee, croissants and the crossword, 'bout my limit.

Slight pause.

HARPER. Well, I don't, I mean, at home. Just porridge or some cornflakes.

He gestures at his breakfast.

Treat.

CLIFFORD *smiles.*

CLIFFORD. Well, it's a filthy Yankee habit, breakfast meetings, but I thought . . . Worthwhile.

Slight pause.

HARPER. So what's your view, the score so far?

CLIFFORD. 'Bout equal. Union and strikers. P'raps the latter, just ahead on points. Since all the rumpus.

HARPER. Us?

CLIFFORD. We're where I wanted us to be.

HARPER. Which is?

CLIFFORD. Not on the field at all. Observers. Watch the game. Or, p'raps a better way of putting it, a kind of referee.

HARPER. That's how you want it?

CLIFFORD. Yes.

Slight pause.

Do you?

HARPER. Not sure. No, I suppose, in this, you're right.

CLIFFORD. In this?

HARPER. In this affair. I'm thinking really . . .

CLIFFORD. Yes?

HARPER. About the wider thing.

Pause.

CLIFFORD. What wider thing?

Pause.

HARPER. You know, Nick, in this area, the textile business, twined around its heart. Defines the place. What's good for worsted, so they say, is good for the West Riding. Mean, they treat the going rate for wool tops like the weather forecast. Even now.

CLIFFORD *smiles.*

You know, there was a time, this industry, when bosses knew their workers, all of them, by name. That's when that didn't mean a working grasp of Arabic.

HARPER *smiles.* CLIFFORD *half-smiles.*

You know, there's – in the boardroom, there's these portraits, of these stern old gentlemen, my grandfather, great grandfather. All rich and heavy.

And there's my uncle, and my father, he took over, when my uncle died in Normandy, in 1944. And he, p'raps not so stern – benign. Still firm, still very much in charge, but more benign.

Slight pause.

Then at the end. A kind of afterthought. There isn't really room for it, wedged in between my uncle and the window frame, there's me.

Slight pause.

And when you look at it, it's got a sort of silly smile. Kind of apologetic. S'if the painter knew – my picture was the last.

CLIFFORD *embarrassed.*

CLIFFORD. Isn't your son?

HARPER. My son's at LSE. He's reading Economics. Wants to be a teacher. Hates the north. He wants to teach, in somewhere proletarian, like Bethnal Green.

Pause.

That's not the point. Not what my son . . . The point is that my industry is dying.

Pause.

It's difficult, therefore, to stand back and observe.

Pause.

I better go. I want to slip up to the works. I'll see you there.

He stands.

There's only one way for this business to survive, you know. Only one way.

CLIFFORD *looks up, questioning.*

The new technology, of course. And something else. Secure and stable workforce. Not people work a year or two and bugger off for better pay. Or leave it altogether. Need . . . Commitment. Discipline . . . And any firm who's got that, will survive.

Slight pause.

The rest of us . . .

CLIFFORD (*quietly*). Oh, come on, Eric . . .

HARPER. You know, I welcome this Inquiry. Actually. Not cos of what's been said. So far, I mean. What could be said. About the real, facts of life.

Slight pause.

Perhaps . . . it's after all, your job, to stop me saying them. I'll see you there.

He goes out. CLIFFORD *puzzled. Then he shrugs, picks up his paper. Then he pours another coffee, but the pot is empty. Calls:*

Um, waitress – ? Miss?

Pause. Lights change.

Scene Eighteen

The Court.

CHAIR, JOWETT, WATTS, SANDHU, HUSSEIN, RIDLEEY, CLIFFORD, CHAIR.

CHAIR. Ladies and gentlemen, I would like to begin this morning with Mrs Anshuya Ridley of the Manchester Community Relations Council, but before that, I have been told by Mr Jowett that he wishes to make a short statement.

JOWETT. Thank you. I think it's obvious what this arises from.
    Madam Chairman, we in the National Union of Weavers have an inter-racial membership. We have a lot of white people, some brown people and one or two black people. In the winter we have blue people and in summer some of our members lie on beaches and turn bright red. Now we could pursue a policy of unequal treatment of any of these hues, but we believe that a worker is a worker is a worker, and we reject discrimination against any members, wherever that discrimination may come from. As far as humanly possible, we have been, are now and intend to remain a colour-blind organisation. That's it.

CHAIR. I'm sure everyone here will welcome that, Mr Jowett. I wonder whether at this point there is anything Mrs Watts wishes to say on behalf of the strike committee.

Slight pause.

WATTS. Well, I would say . . .

Her eye catches SANDHU'S.

That on this side we agree with your statement that an atmosphere of reason is preferable to one of irrationality.

Pause.

CHAIR. Yes. I see.
    Let us move on. I had hoped, in view of Mr Faruqi's complaint, that we would have a representative of the Race Relations Board of the Inquiry. However, sadly, the officer concerned is overseas at the moment. Mrs Ridley has agreed, however, to comment on the role of the Board in a general way, and in a broad sense to represent what is known in the jargon as the Race Relations Industry. Mrs Ridley, I am afraid you can have had no more than a cursory glance through yesterday's transcript, but I wonder if there's anything you'd like to say?

RIDLEY. Well, I don't think I wish to make any general statement. There are however a couple of specific points I'd like to touch upon.

CHAIR. Please.

RIDLEY. They both concern the matter of my feeling that the move to an integrated production situation would remove many of the potential areas of tension and division. While this appears to have been accepted, there seems to be an impression that I was unmindful of the redundancy implications. I must state unequivocally that this is not so. It was made quite clear to me that an additional element – the retention of some dayshift jobs – would be part of any new package, and it was also made plain that the choice was either a new package or the firm's collapse.

The second point is an obvious one. It was not of course in my mind that the new scheme would be presented while most of the Asian workforce was on strike.

CHAIR. Thank you. Are there any comments on this?

CLIFFORD. Yes, a couple, Madam Chairman. The first is to repeat that while the second strike may not have been in Mrs Ridley's mind, it was not, of course, in the company's mind either.

The second point is that there was a proposal raised at one point that the company should introduce some kind of quota system for Asian promotion. This was not considered appropriate and I wonder if Mrs Ridley could comment on this.

RIDLEY. This is answered simply. It is not, to use counsel's words, inappropriate to introduce a quota system. It is illegal under the terms of the Act.

CLIFFORD. I see.

CHAIR. Mr Clifford, do you have anything else?

CLIFFORD. Well, only to hope that Mrs Ridley will comment on the fact that the company was found not guilty of discrimination under the Race Relations Act.

RIDLEY. Yes. Can I preface this by explaining that there are two statutory bodies concerned with Race Relations. One is the Community Relations Commission, which I represent, and which has no legal powers. The Race Relations Board, on the other hand, has the job of implementing the 1968 Race Relations Act. I have worked for the Board in the past, and have read its report in this case.

CHAIR. I can ask you to comment, but I cannot press you to do so.

RIDLEY. I can make a comment, in a general way. There are three reasons, I think, why this complaint failed. The first, frankly, concerns the very nature of the legislation, which stipulates that no investigation can take place unless there has been a complaint from an individual. Obviously, in a case like this, there are a larger number of individual grievances, which built up into a general pattern for the minority group, but the Board is only empowered to deal with the individual matter brought to its attention, which may, in isolation, not appear so grave.

CHAIR. This is really the point made yesterday about the company's own procedure.

RIDLEY. Yes, I think I spotted that. The second point is more specific. According to the Board, the main complaint was about compulsory overtime. Unfortunately, this was held not to be discriminatory because the workers had accepted it voluntarily.

CHAIR. Mrs Ridley, are you saying that if a racial minority as it were agrees to be put in an inferior position, then that is not discrimination?

RIDLEY. Under the terms of the Act, no. It is a general deficiency of this type of legislation. Another vivid example is recruitment. Obviously, many black and coloured people do not apply for certain jobs when they have been told, or fear, that they will meet prejudice. In such a case, they are, of course, victims of discrimination in a very real sense. But if they do not actually face concrete rejection, then, in legal terms, it does not exist.

CHAIR. Let me get this clear. If there was a situation where a racial minority – or even a majority – were as it were prevented by entrenched custom and practice from work in certain areas, and therefore never bothered to apply, knowing there'd be no chance of getting a job, then that would not be held to be discrimination?

RIDLEY. I see exactly where you're heading, Madam Chairman. Yes. It is true, that on the face of it, the Race Relations Act 1968 would find it extremely hard to find racial discrimination in the Republic of South Africa.

CLIFFORD. Madam, this is all highly instructive, but it does not alter the fact that the Board found that no discrimination had occurred in this case.

RIDLEY. Well, it found that no discrimination had occurred under the Act. It's really a reverse of the old joke that the only person who can prove they are sane is the person who has a certificate of dismissal from a mental hospital. Now, the company has a kind of certificate saying that it has not contravened the law. This doesn't mean that it has not discriminated. This is another reason why people tend to be circumspect about using the law in these cases.

CHAIR. Mrs Ridley, do I detect a point of inter-departmental rivalry here?

RIDLEY. Of course you detect no such thing, Madam Chairman. It is, however, true that I now work for an organisation that muddles along quite happily without recourse to statutory powers.

CHAIR. You said there was a third reason for the failure of Mr Faruqi's complaint?

RIDLEY. Oh, indeed. From the report it is clear that the Board received a marked lack of cooperation from one of the parties involved?

CHAIR. This was the company?

RIDLEY. No, the company was quite helpful. The party concerned was the strike committee. They refused to see the Board.

CHAIR. But it was a member of the strike committee who made the complaint in the first place.

RIDLEY. Yes.

WATTS. Madam Chairman, I think what has emerged in the last few minutes demonstrates quite clearly why the Asian workers were unwilling to cooperate with the Board.

CHAIR. Well, yes, but that doesn't explain why Mr Faruqi made the complaint in the first place.

WATTS. May I consult a moment?

CHAIR. Of course.

WATTS *talks to* HUSSEIN *and* SANDHU.

WATTS. I think the best way of putting it would be to say that there was a disagreement on tactics. Mr Faruqi made his complaint, of course, before the strike began. By the time the Board got round to investigating it, the strikers felt themselves to be, using an Americanism, in a whole new ball-game.

DAWSON *laughs*.

CHAIR (*sharply*). Mrs Dawson, do you have a comment?

DAWSON. No, I have no comment.

CHAIR. Mrs Ridley, is there anything you'd like to say in conclusion?

RIDLEY. Yes, briefly.

I think that anyone who works in what you called the Race Relations Industry is aware that there are no easy panaceas for the problems of communities living together. There are wide cultural differences, which it is foolish and not a little romantic to deny.

But, having said that, I think the revelation of disagreement within the Asians themselves is, in a paradoxical way, rather encouraging. Because it shows that the minority workforce is a group of people with individual concerns and priorities, just like any other group. In the same way, the fact that a largish number returned to work during the second strike, while this might seem regrettable in some ways, is at least an indication that the mill is not irreversibly divided on racial lines. It is, I am sure, our hope that the indigenous workforce will not feel that they must act like a tribe in defence of their interests, and one way to prevent that is for the minority communities not to operate in a tribal fashion either.

I think that's all I have to say.

CHAIR. Thank you . . . I wonder, before you go, if you could repeat one point you made.

RIDLEY. Yes?

CHAIR. Did you say a large number of Asians returned to work during the second strike?

RIDLEY. Well, I was not involved at that stage, of course, but I had gathered that that was the case.

CHAIR. This I think is new.

WATTS *whispering with the strikers*.

JOWETT. Perhaps I could . . .

CHAIR. Yes of course.

JOWETT. Broadly, what happened: it was during the second week of the second stoppage. The Asians had come out on Thursday the 29th May. The following Tuesday and Wednesday, the third and fourth of June, a largish number, I mean, 20 or so, came back.

CHAIR. Were these perhaps people not directly involved?

JOWETT. Well, some. But a lot were nightshift workers. It was this, frankly, led us to think there might be, shall we say, external influences at work.

CHAIR. People like Mr Kadir?

JOWETT. People, like that, yes.

CHAIR. Can I ask why you didn't mention this before?

JOWETT. Well . . . I think . . . I don't agree with this strike. I never have. But, on the other hand I'm not one to volunteer the fact a strike's not solid. You could say it goes against the grain.

CHAIR. Mrs Watts, there must be some comment on this.

WATTS. I am instructed that what Mr Jowett says is more or less so. A number did return.

CHAIR. Why?

WATTS. Well, to be frank, one reason was that there were families, extended families, whose only breadwinner worked at the mill, or whose only source of income was perhaps two or three family members working. In these cases, the committee did let a few people continue to work, on compassionate grounds.

CHAIR. Yes, I see that, but we're not talking about people continuing to work. We're talking about people returning to work, if I may say so, in droves.

WATTS. Another factor, of course, may have been the issue of dismissal notices. This precipitous act –

CHAIR. Well, I'm sorry, that doesn't work either. Mr Jowett said the return was on the second and third. The dismissal notices weren't sent out till the fourth.

WATTS (*after a pause*). Madam Chairman, I'm afraid I am going to have to take further instructions.

CHAIR. Do I take is that there is another factor in all this?

WATTS. I'm afraid I have to take instructions.

CHAIR. Very well. I was planning a short adjournment. We will take it now.

Lights change.

Scene Nineteen

Canteen.

Enter WATTS *followed by* HUSSEIN *and* SANDHU.

WATTS. Well, I'm sorry, but I think you're berserk.

SANDHU. So you keep saying.

They sit, as:

WATTS. What on earth will we gain?

SANDHU. What do you think?

WATTS. Tell me.

SANDHU. We'll gain by making clear why we will not work with the Race Relations Industry. We'll gain by making clear why Mr Jowett's white and black and blue and crimson workers is just –

WATTS. Ranjit. We're talking about what is, I mean, don't get me wrong, I'm dead opposed to it, but we are talking now about a criminal offence. Offences.

SANDHU. Oh dear.

WATTS. Yes? Oh dear what?

SANDHU. Oh dear you're all the same. This fetish with the law. You're all the same.

WATTS. When you say 'you' –

SANDHU. White liberals.

HUSSEIN. Ranjit.

Pause.

WATTS. I can't stop you. You employ me. And whatever you may think of how I'm doing this, or what I am, I will do what you want.

Pause.

HUSSEIN. We think that this thing must be brought out.

WATTS. I disagree with you, but we will do it. Right?

SANDHU. And there's the other matter.

WATTS. Oh, yes. That. Well, once again, I must say my advice is –

SANDHU. Look, we know about it, it's quite common knowledge, been on all their marches, been –

WATTS stops SANDHU *with a gesture. She has noticed* KITCHEN *and* DAWSON *have entered.*

WATTS. Shall we adjourn, find somewhere quiet?

HUSSEIN. Yes, let's do that.

WATTS, HUSSEIN *and* SANDHU *go out.*

KITCHEN. What's it all about d'you s'pose?

DAWSON. Well, I dunno, do I?

Pause.

KITCHEN. I see them two last night.

DAWSON. Oh, ay?

KITCHEN. I talked to them.

DAWSON. That's nice.

KITCHEN. No, weren't. Bloody edgy. Fact, they was bloody rude.

DAWSON. You shatter me.

Slight pause.

KITCHEN. Just wondered why, that's all.

DAWSON. What d'you mean, you wondered why?

KITCHEN. The tone of voice, you know, the style of talking. Déjà vu.

DAWSON. Frank, I don't speak foreign languages. S'why I find working Darley Park so –

KITCHEN. Sounded just like I do when I'm locked in some great barney with the management. A kind of, sullen. Sarkey. Clever. And distrustful.

Slight pause. Lighter.

Just don't expect to hear it used at you. I'll go and get some coffee.

He goes out.

DAWSON. Frank –

DAWSON *looks after for a moment. Then she looks at the table where the strikers were sitting.*

You go ahead.

Blackout.

Scene Twenty

The Court.

CHAIR, WATTS, DAWSON, SANDHU, HUSSEIN, JOWETT, KITCHEN.

WATTS. Madam, I asked for time to consult on this question, and the reason was that I felt that certain matters involved would be counter-productive to the strikers' case. I have put this point of view, but have failed to convince those who are instructing me. I must therefore ask you to let Mr Hussein make a statement. I should also say that Mr Hussein will shed light on why, as I said yesterday, Abdul Kadir is unable to assist this Inquiry.

CHAIR. Mr Hussein.

HUSSEIN. Um, Madam, the position is this. Although most of the picket line trouble occurred recently, a few arrests did happen during the first strike. One of the people arrested was Abdul Kadir, on the 23rd May. He was, um –

WATTS. Remanded.

HUSSEIN. He was remanded on bail to appear in court some time in early June, charged with threatening abuse or some such charge.

Slight pause.

However, on 1st of June, a Sunday, Mr Kadir was arrested at his home for a different offence. He was taken in custody and was later transferred to a prison in the south of England. To await deportation.

CHAIR. Deportation? Why?

HUSSEIN. Because he was, it was claimed he was an illegal immigrant. A student overstayer. Stopped his course, should have gone back. Under the Immigration Act he can be – well, the word's not even deportation. He can be 'removed'.

CHAIR. Mr Hussein, I'm still not quite sure how this connects with –

HUSSEIN. Well, I think it is not too hard to comprehend. There is a strike. There are pickets and they are stopping things going in and affecting the company's operation. And then a Pakistani is arrested and he faces being removed. Two or so days later, other Pakistani strikers, in a body, break the strike, go back to work. I think it's not impossible to understand.

CHAIR. You're saying, in effect, that some or all of these strikers were fearful that they too might be arrested as illegal immigrants?

HUSSEIN. Of course.

CHAIR. Then can we conclude that some or all of them are in fact living illegally in this country?

HUSSEIN. Under the 1971 Immigration Act or the Pakistan Act, yes.

CHAIR. Under the law of our land?

HUSSEIN. Yes, under the law of your land.

CHAIR. Thank you. I must say I can understand Mrs Watts' reticence, under the circumstances. But there we are. Before we move on, I must ask a couple of questions. I did detect, I think, an implication that the company had been involved with, had somehow provoked, the arrest of Mr Kadir. As I'm sure this was not the case –

SANDHU. Oh, no, of course, they had nothing to do with it.

CHAIR. I'm glad to hear that, Mr Sandhu.

SANDHU. Cos they don't need to. Any immigrant will tell you. This, machine, it operates without the touch of human hand, it works quite automatically. As it is designed to do.

Pause.

CHAIR. Yes. I'd now like to ask, I think we ought to know, if Mr Jowett and/or Mr Kitchen knew about this?

JOWETT. I think it's fair to say I had an inkling. It's not, again, the sort of thing I'd volunteer.

CHAIR. And Mr Kitchen?

KITCHEN. No.

CHAIR. You mean you –

KITCHEN. I'd no idea at all.

CHAIR. Thank you. I think, now, we must leave the matter there. I now wish to proceed –

SANDHU. But there is another point.

CHAIR. Mr Sandhu, I think unless –

SANDHU. A different point. From Mrs Watts.

CHAIR. Perhaps then she could tell us what it is.

WATTS. Yes, Madam Chairman, there is a further point. It is in fact another point I advised the Committee not to pursue, in this case on the grounds that you might find it inadmissible. But once again, I have been over-ruled.
  The argument, the point is really that, as, already we have moved, or been dragged, into what you could call a more political situation . . .

CHAIR. Mrs Watts, I think it would help your point if you came to it.

WATTS. Well, it concerns, in brief, the political affiliations of a member of the factory Committee.

CHAIR. Then your advice was correct. I would be most unhappy –

WATTS. Yes, well I must put their argument, and say that in this case the matter is of relevance.

CHAIR. And I must disagree with you.

WATTS. Then I must ask, if you would be prepared, perhaps, to admit this evidence in camera.

CHAIR. Well, even then, I would be most –

DAWSON. Don't bother.

CHAIR. What?

DAWSON. Don't bother, go in camera. I'll tell you what she's on about.

CHAIR. Well, I'm –

DAWSON. She's on about me being in the Front.

  Pause.

CHAIR. By 'Front', you mean, the National –

JOWETT. Madam Chairman, I'm not a lawyer, and I don't know how you're supposed to make objections, but –

DAWSON (*interrupts*). Cos I have sat here for two days and heard everyone being very polite and very reasonable and very friendly. And no-one's been so vulgar as to say there might be sides, and some on one and others on the other.

Now, perhaps, it's time that things came out, a bit, into the open.

And I won't be long, promise. Cos she's already said it. Far as I'm concerned, Mrs Highgate Village said it. The employers and the coloureds on the same, same side. Well, begin to ask some questions. Don't you? Then.

Cos far as I'm concerned, she's right. They are the other side. We are our side.

Slight pause.

But, of course, aye, can't be. Cos they are the oppressed. And bosses are oppressors. How they stop you seeing. That the people called exploiters and exploited are the same. They say, the bosses and the communists are locked in struggle for the world. They stop you seeing that it's bankers and financiers who give the money to the communists. See how it's them encourages this lot to come here. Live here. Breed. And inter-breed.

It's a conspiracy. No doubt in my mind. It's a conspiracy, to undermine our race. By bringing them. By other things. The unemployment. Common Market. Mucky magazines. The general . . . rot. Pollute our nation from within.

It's all connected. Seems quite clear to me. Destroy the nation. Then take over everything. You see?

Slight pause.

I hadn't seen it, quite that . . . Hadn't seen before.

Pause.

Well now, if you'll forgive me. Suddenly, don't feel too good. As may be obvious, I'm in what you could call a pregnant situation.

DAWSON *stands and goes out.*

CHAIR. Well –

KITCHEN. Madam Chairman, I'd like to ask something.

CHAIR *waves him on.*

I think – I'd like to ask, Mr Hussein or Mr Sandhu. What I want to ask is, why they told us. 'Bout their people being illegal immigrants. I'd like to ask them that.

CHAIR. Would – one of you . . .

HUSSEIN. Well. Mr Jowett said earlier that a worker is a worker is a worker. White or black or brown or green with yellow stripes. Mrs Ridley said earlier that we should be the same as other workers. Don't be a tribe and they won't be a tribe.

Slight pause.

But we are not the same as other workers. Because white workers do not have to take their passports when they go to work. That is the point.

We are not like whites because they are not working side-by-side with people who desire to put them all on boats to go back where they did or didn't come from. That's the point.

Pause.

We are not over here because of some great conspiracy. We are over here because you wanted us to come here. We are over here because, dear Mr Kitchen, you were over there.

SANDHU. And if they divide us, they're dividing you.

Blackout.

Scene Twenty-One

Canteen.

DAWSON *sits.* BHANDARI *and* SANDHU *cross the stage. They look at* DAWSON, *she doesn't look back. At exit,* SANDHU *goes out, but* BHANDARI *stops and turns back. She gives a little cough. No reaction. She tries again.* DAWSON *looks up.*

DAWSON. Want something?

BHANDARI. No.

DAWSON. Right.

BHANDARI. Wondered, you might want something.

DAWSON. Like what?

BHANDARI. Some dinner, something.

DAWSON. Being got some, thanks.

BHANDARI. You OK now?

DAWSON. I'm wonderful.

Slight pause.

Well. Don't let me detain you. Sure you've got lots to be getting on with. Planning tactics with your friend the whirling dervish.

Slight pause. BHANDARI *smiles.*

BHANDARI. Dervish? You mean Ranjit Sandhu? Oh, he's OK. Shows off, you know.

DAWSON. You what?

BHANDARI. He likes to think he's tough. But underneath, no way.

DAWSON. Oh, ay?

BHANDARI. He once – he saw us, women on the picket line, it scared the pants off him. He said.

DAWSON. Oh, did he?

BHANDARI. Yes.

Slight pause.

DAWSON. I doubt that many of your menfolk were that shot on your activities.

BHANDARI. Now that is true. That's very true.

DAWSON *looks in some surprise as* BHANDARI *continues chattily.*

A lot of them, you know their husbands said, when they said they were on picket duty, said, oh you can't do that. With all those men. Stay home, my girl, and catch up on the laundry. Can't have you going on all hours striking. What about the cooking and the home? And, even worse, we went collecting and a lot of husbands, fathers, they said: that's begging. And of course that's very bad. Oh, no, a lot of them said, they don't approve at all.

Slight pause.

I s'pose, your husband, might react the same, if you came out on strike.

DAWSON. I doubt it. Rather different, i'n't it, Asian women. Subjugated. Kept in purdah. Kept behind locked doors. I wonder, what they thought of Madam Ridley. Married to a white. I bet that went against the grain. I bet that went down like a cup of sick.

BHANDARI. Well, surely, it's the same the other way.

DAWSON. Keep them locked up. Don't want them, get polluted by our filthy Western ways.

BHANDARI. Oh, not just Western ways. In fact, it's happening in India and Pakistan. Women campaigning. 'Gainst arranging marriages. Fighting for rights. In fact, it's not just here.

Slight pause.

But it is harder here. Because if you do not belong inside your own community, there's nowhere else you can belong.

DAWSON. Go home then. If it's harder here. Go back to where you came from.

BHANDARI. If I go back where I came from, I get shot.

DAWSON. You what?

BHANDARI. Uganda.

Slight pause.

DAWSON. Hm. You know, funny, in't it. Any place you got two races. Never mix. The blacks don't want the Asians in Uganda, and now I come to think of it, round here there's one or –

BHANDARI. Uganda, it was not the blacks who made divisions.

DAWSON. Who, then?

BHANDARI. Was the British. Put the Asians in, to run the blacks. Because Uganda is a little bit too hot for white men. So they put the Asians in, to run things for them. No surprise, what happened, don't you think?

Pause.

DAWSON. Well, you're all right now, aren't you? Now we've welcomed you with open arms.

BHANDARI (*smiles*). They didn't look that open in the camps. They didn't look that open for the husbands without British passports, shuttled round the world.

Pause.

DAWSON. Well, this is most illuminating, but –

BHANDARI. D'you meant that, what you said in there? About an international conspiracy?

DAWSON. Of course I mean it. Said it, didn't I? There's people who would like to see our race destroyed.

BHANDARI. Bankers, you said. Financiers.

DAWSON. That's right.

BHANDARI. You know, that's very interesting.

DAWSON. Why.

BHANDARI. Cos that is just what is said by our own President Amin. Only he's a little more specific. Says it is the Jews.

Slight pause. DAWSON *moves to stand.* KITCHEN *has appeared with* DAWSON's *dinner, stands behind her.*

Don't you, really . . . You say the race. You are not, p'raps, before you are an English person, first of all a worker? Or perhaps a woman?

DAWSON. First, I'm a white woman. First, I'm a white worker.

BHANDARI. Mm. Sometimes, you know, I think . . .

DAWSON. Yuh? What d'you think?

BHANDARI. That they give you whiteness so that you can put up with the rest. They give you such a dreadful life, but say, at least you're white. At least, in that, you are superior.
You know, if you're the bottom of the pile, the real dregs, black woman . . . We've grown up, through this strike. We won't put up with dreadful things, now, any more. From overlookers. Husbands. Foremen. Fathers. You.

DAWSON. Well, I'm very sorry, love, but frankly I can't give a toss about your home-life or your strike.

BHANDARI (*suddenly hard*). Then we were right. You are a chancha.

DAWSON. Sorry, don't speak Urdu.

BHANDARI. Gujerati. Scab.

She makes to go.

KITCHEN. You should have –

BHANDARI *turns back.*

You should have said all that in there.

DAWSON. So what?

BHANDARI. We're not brought up to say too much out loud.

She goes out.

DAWSON. Frank? Frank?

KITCHEN (*giving her the food*). Your dinner.

DAWSON. Ta. Where's yours?

KITCHEN. Not hungry. Got to have a word with someone.

DAWSON. Someone being who?

KITCHEN. You'll see.

DAWSON puts down her dinner, stands.

DAWSON. Frank, for Christ's sake, not getting sentimental?

KITCHEN. Sentimental?

DAWSON. Brotherhood of man. That lot.

KITCHEN. Oh no. Not brotherhood of man. Far from it. Naked, crude self-interest. Not just mine and all.

He makes to go.

DAWSON. Eh, Frank. Is this your bloody déjà vu?

KITCHEN. I'm sorry. Don't speak Urdu. Love.

Blackout.

Scene Twenty-Two

The Court.

CHAIR, WATTS, KITCHEN, HARPER, DAWSON.
WATTS *is reading a hastily scribbled piece of paper.*

CHAIR. Ladies and gentlemen, we are now approaching the stage of final speeches. I have asked Mr Jowett and Mr Clifford if they have any further questions or comments before they sum up, and they have said they are satisfied. Mrs Watts, is there anything else from you at this point?

WATTS. Well, I'm afraid there is, Madam Chairman. It's a matter, or shall I say a perspective, that has only just, as it were, sprung to my notice.

CHAIR. Then you must spring it on us.

WATTS *is not quite sure what she is doing, but she begins confidently.*

WATTS. What I have to say relates really to what has become something of a hardy perennial in this Inquiry: the history of the various Sultzer transfer schemes. Now we have here three events. The first is the initial agreement of 1971, which, as you said, was a splendid deal from management's point of view. We then had what was described as the union's much more belligerent line in 1973 and their final acceptance a month or so ago of the deal they'd rejected in 1973, compulsory redundancies and all.

CHAIR. But with the promised retention of some Dobcross dayshift jobs.

WATTS. Yes.

WATTS *looks at* KITCHEN, *who is looking sepulchral.*

As you will remember, the reason given for the change in the workers' attitude was that in 1973 the industry was in a buoyant state, whereas in 1971 it was fairly depressed.

CHAIR. I recall Mr Jowett said, you win some and you lose some.

WATTS. Indeed. But I would point out, that it is possible, indeed it is really much more likely, that those economic factors would in fact operate in a different way. It is when an industry is in recession that workers can be expected strenuously to protect their jobs, whereas in a time of expansion, there are wider job opportunities in general, and they may regard redundancy less seriously. In other words, it could be argued that the union's reaction to the question of redundancy on these two occasions was, in theory, precisely the wrong way round.
    I wonder, now, could I ask Mr Harper a question?

CHAIR. Yes, of course . . . Mrs Watts, are you quite sure where you're going?

WATTS. Oh, I hope so, Madam Chairman . . . Mr Harper, I wonder if you can remember when in 1973 the transfer negotiations occurred? I mean, the month?

HARPER. Well, they started in late September, broke down in early November.

WATTS (*unsure of herself*). Now, we know, of course, that something else happened in the same year, which was the white worker being appointed as a time-weaver on the nightshift, and the

protests, and your having to promote an Asian; can you tell me
when that happened?

HARPER. To the best of my recollection, that chain of events
occurred in mid-October.

Pause. WATTS *clicks.*

WATTS. Oh, I see.

Pause.

Oh, I see. There must have been . . .

CHAIR. Uh, Mrs Watts . . .

KITCHEN *has had his finger raised for a few moments.*

WATTS. I'm so sorry, Madam Chairman, but I've only just, um . . .

KITCHEN *coughs.*

CHAIR. Yes, Mr Kitchen, you have caught my eye, but unless your
point's germane –

KITCHEN. Oh, it's germane all right.

WATTS, *with a knowingly expansive gesture towards* KITCHEN, *sits.*
DAWSON *looking at* KITCHEN *in alarm.* CHAIR *sizes up.*

CHAIR. Go on.

KITCHEN (*slow and cool*). What, Mrs Watts's come up with, not
before time, is that things broke down, two year ago, cos the
company had broke their side of the agreement.

CHAIR. Sorry, which agreement?

KITCHEN. The 1971 agreement.

CHAIR. Oh, yes, you mean they broke their side of it by asking for
compulsory redundancies? You mean that bit?

KITCHEN. Well, no, not quite that bit. The bit about promotion.

CHAIR. What bit about promotion?

KITCHEN. The bit that said, we'd buy the transfer, with no strings,
if we could have it guaranteed there wouldn't be no Asians made
time-weaver.

CHAIR. Sorry?

KITCHEN. Cos, 'course, the transfer happens, and we're all
together, i'n't we. On the Sultzers. Spread throughout the mill,
our sunburned brethren. And there's bright lads, 'mong the

Pakkies, sooner, later, bound to get the leg-up. So we said, no
guarantee, no deal.

And everything were fine. Till two year ago. We're
renegotiating. What they do? Promote a darky, don't they. OK,
on the nightshift, and that's as black as ink. But once they set a
precedent . . . D'be the Sultzers. One. And then another. Then
another. So we says, no way. The transfer stops, right now.

That's all.

CHAIR. I had been under the impression that it was something to do
with preventing redundancies among the women weavers.

KITCHEN. Oh, ay, and that as well.

CHAIR. Now let me get this straight –

KITCHEN (*slightly impatient*). There was a deal. No black time-
weavers. Deal, with management, so they could get their
precious Sultzers in. Not written down. Not formal. Shall we
say, a gentleman's agreement.

Pause.

CHAIR. Can I ask why you've said this now?

KITCHEN. Oh, yuh. A reasonable question. Cos it was a lousy deal.
Because of what we lost. Because the thing was bad right
through.

CHAIR. You mean, ethically?

KITCHEN. Practically. Bad, for us.

He looks to DAWSON. *He stands. As he speaks, he writes something
on a piece of paper.*

Well, I don't know if you was planning breaking this, but I need
a cup of tea.

He gives WATTS *the piece of paper and goes out. Pause.*

WATTS. Um, Madam Chairman, the fact that members of the white
workforce are opposed to Asian timeweavers is not news.

CHAIR. No, it isn't. Perhaps, Mr Harper . . .

During some of the following, WATTS *puzzles over the piece of paper.*
KITCHEN *has given her. She gradually realises what it means, and
makes a few notes.*

HARPER. Well, Madam Chairman, really, none of this is very new.

CHAIR. In what way, Mr Harper? It seems quite novel to me.

HARPER. Well, I mean, this atmosphere of, shall I say, melodrama and dénouement. We've acknowledged all along that there would be resistance to promoting Asians.

CHAIR. But the point is, Mr Kitchen said that you were party to a deal –

HARPER. I wouldn't say a deal.

CHAIR. What would you say?

HARPER. More, an acknowledgement of the facts of life.

CHAIR. But there is a difference between acknowledging a fact, if fact it is –

HARPER. Oh, it's fact all right –

CHAIR. And making it part of an agreement.

HARPER. I wouldn't say it was entirely part of our agreement.

CHAIR. Mr Harper, was there, or was there not, a deal, arrangement, understanding, what you like, that if you didn't promote Asians, that then and only then would the white workers accept the transfer scheme?

Pause.

HARPER. If we'd promoted Asians, as we wished, on merit and experience, then we'd have had a walk-out. Now I don't like that, any more than you, but it was just accepting an accomplished fact.

CHAIR. Mr Harper, 50 Asians walked out seven weeks ago. That was accomplished and it's still a fact. Now you have said you gave into white pressure to avoid disruption. Now there does seem to be some kind of double-standard operating here. To put it mildly.

Slight pause.

Now I must ask you once again, if there was what Mr Kitchen calls a gentlemen's agreement on promotion to which you as management were party?

HARPER. I'm saying we acknowledged what the situation was. That's all.

WATTS *has worked everything out.*

WATTS. Madam Chairman, just one point.

CHAIR. Yes?

WATTS. It's about the final offer, the new scheme, accepted on the 18th of June, the one that was explained by Mr Jowett as the workers running out of rope.

CHAIR. Yes?

WATTS. I'd just like to ask Mr Harper to remind us how many jobs will be retained for Dobcross dayshift workers.

HARPER. There will be eight jobs retained.

WATTS. Then can I ask, if voluntary redundancy were to continue at an expected rate, would you expect there would be enough natural wastage to reduce the dayshift from its present twenty-five to eight?

HARPER. No. I'd say, we'd need actually to dismiss around, say, ten. But this was made quite clear –

WATTS. Madam Chairman, the white workers, including, for it was a virtually unanimous decision, the white women, accepted on the 18th of June a deal that would we've heard, require about ten compulsory redundancies on the Dobcross dayshift alone. It seems very odd that they should accept that, rope or no rope, until you remember that six days earlier eleven Asian women, who otherwise would have competed for those eight jobs, were sacked for having gone on strike.

CHAIR. Yes. I see the point.

WATTS. Now I am tempted, I am very tempted, to ask Mrs Dawson a question or two about that.

She picks up KITCHEN's *piece of paper.*

But I shall refrain from doing so, because I have another question for Mr Harper, which may put the matter in a different perspective. I wonder if Mr Harper has the actual text of the new scheme to hand.

CHAIR. Mr Harper?

HARPER (*finds it*). Yes.

WATTS. And could he read the actual clause about the eight Dobcross jobs.

HARPER. Well, I think this is the one. 'It is further agreed that a minimum of eight dayshift jobs shall be preserved on the remaining Dobcross looms'.

CHAIR. When you say a minimum?

HARPER. I must confess that also means a maximum.

CHAIR. Yes, I see. Mrs Watts, I'm sorry, what exactly is the –

Click.

Mr Harper, read that again.

HARPER. Um . . . 'It is further agreed that a minimum of eight dayshift jobs shall be preserved on the remaining Dobcross looms'.

CHAIR. It doesn't say jobs for women.

Pause.

HARPER. So it doesn't.

CHAIR. It could mean men? Male jobs?

HARPER. Well, yes, it could.

CHAIR. Does it?

HARPER. Eventually.

Pause.

CHAIR. Can I ask why?

HARPER. Well, you of all people should know that, Madam Chairman.

CHAIR. Continue.

HARPER. I mean, you're going to be on it, so I read.

CHAIR. On what?

HARPER. The Equal Opportunities Commission.

Pause.

WATTS. It's now July 1975. The transfer takes, say, a year. On the first of January 1976, the Equal Pay act comes into force.

CHAIR. Mr Harper, you said, or implied, that you hoped to see an all-male weaving workforce, I think you said 'eventually'. How soon is eventually?

HARPER. Eventually is, frankly, as soon as possible. A year at most.

Pause.

Look, it's just the facts. That if you've got to pay the same . . . You lose the flexibility, they can't be moved to shifts . . . And, frankly, it does cost to train them. And then, they do, get married. Pregnant.

Slight pause.

Nothing I can do, to change the facts of life.

DAWSON *stands and quickly goes out.*

CHAIR. Mrs Watts, curiosity has got the better of me. What was on the piece of paper Mr Kitchen gave you?

WATTS. Oh, just . . . what he wrote was: 'Glory be. All this and Maggie Thatcher too.'

CHAIR. I'm sorry.

WATTS. Just a private joke.

Lights change.

Scene Twenty-Three

The Court.
  The final speeches.
  Spot on CLIFFORD.

CLIFFORD. Madam Chairman, the company believes that this Inquiry has shown it to be, in many ways, the pig-in-the middle of this affair, crushed between the irresistible force of the Asian workers' demands on the one hand, and the immovable object of the indigenous weavers' fears on the other.

Spot off CLIFFORD. *Spot on* JOWETT.

JOWETT. Madam Chairman, the union takes the view that events of the last couple of days show it to have been the ham-in-the-sandwich in all of this. It is the union that has been trying to mediate between the Asians' insistence on better pay and conditions, and the company's refusal to yield to those demands.

Lights change.

Spot off JOWETT. *Spot on* WATTS.

WATTS. Madam Chairman, I think it is now clear, whatever the Race Relations Board may have concluded, that there has been a legacy of systematic and conscious racialism at Darley Park Mill. It is up to you to decide on the causes of this, but I would like to suggest a possible perspective.

In the late 1960s, like many other companies, the management of Darley Park took on immigrant labour to perform jobs that indigenous workers were unprepared to do. These jobs involved low pay, bad conditions and unsocial hours. While the immigrants were prepared to aquiesce in this, it was in the company's interests to preserve divisions between the immigrant and indigenous workforces. Specifically, the company was sure that if certain privileges were preserved for the white workers, then those workers would be content to allow the continued exploitation, or I might say super-exploitation, of the Asian workforce, whether or not this undermined agreements and practices that the union has struggled over many years to secure. This was, I would submit, the background of the shabby, and aptly-named gentleman's agreement that Mr Kitchen had the courage to reveal to us earlier today.

However, this kind of arrangement was only satisfactory to the company while the Asian workforce was prepared to accept its situation. Two years ago, the Asians as it were gave notice that it was no longer prepared to be super-exploited, and in the last seven weeks it has confirmed its new militancy in no uncertain terms. The advantages of continued racial division between the workers, from the company's point of view, disappeared at the moment when the Asians insisted on their right to be promoted equally with whites, and demonstrated its willingness and capacity to fight. From that point onwards, it was in the interests of the company to support a liberal and progressive policy against the shopfloor racialism that it had itself created. In short, the company had built a monster which then went way beyond control, and it is now denying its own creature.

The consequences of this seem clear. The victims of this sorry saga are not going to be white men, or even, probably, Asian men. They are going to be white and Asian women. The divisions between white and black – which the union allowed to grow and then insisted be retained – have in their turn allowed the firm to drive a further wedge, a wedge affecting black and white, between the men and women in the company.

Madam Chairman, I have one final point, and, if you'll forgive me, this does go back quite far into history. Over a hundred years ago, during the American Civil War, Lancashire textile workers refused to work cotton that had been imported from the Southern States. The workers were in many cases starving, and were offered high wages to spin the cotton, but they refused to do so as an act of solidarity with black slaves fighting for their freedom. This is not, of course, an isolated case. The British Labour Movement has always had a strong and noble tradition of support for the liberation of all people, black and white, from exploitation and oppression. It's my hope that this Inquiry will see that fine tradition brought on home.

Lights change.

Spot off WATTS. *Spot on the* CHAIR.

CHAIR. Thank you, Mrs Watts. It is now my task to produce a report on the evidence that I have heard and to present it to the Secretary of State. I would thank you all for your attendance and your contributions. I declare this hearing closed.

Blackout.

Scene Twenty-Four

Various.
In the darkness.

LOUDSPEAKER (*ting tong*). Flight announcement. Will passengers for TWA Flight 301 for Washington please proceed to Departure Gate 21. Passengers for TWA Washington please proceed to departure gate 21. Thank you. (*ting tong.*)

Lights on a young Pakistani sitting on one of the short row of plastic chairs. His hand luggage is beside him. He is reading a Government report.

LOUDSPEAKER (*ting tong*). Passenger announcement. Will Miss Susan Palmer, passenger recently arrived from Sydney, please report to the Qantas desk in the main concourse. Staff announcement. Will Mr Ramesh Desai please go to the catering managers' office. Thank you. (*ting tong.*)

Lights fade a little on the Pakistani. Light on CLIFFORD *at the desk. on the telephone. The same Government report is open before him.*

CLIFFORD. Mr Harper please, Nicholas Clifford calling.

Pause.

Eric. Nick. Hallo. Have you seen it? Oh, well, you should get it today. In general, from your point of view, it's fairly predictable. Um . . . 'The company in my view showed insufficient courage . . . Unduly timid . . . occasionally unthinking and precipitous . . . errors of judgement . . .'

Slight pause.

Oh, money? Well, I'm afraid she wants an interim bonus and piecework changes. Not all they demanded, but . . .

Pause.

Oh, yes, of course, that hadn't struck me. yes, as you say, since yesterday, a whole new ball-game, with this six pounds limit thing, agreed. Presumably that means that even if you wanted to . . . Yes, indeed. You couldn't break it. After all, it's more or less the law.

Lights off CLIFFORD.

Lights back up on the Pakistani. He lights a cigarette.

LOUDSPEAKER (*ting tong*). Flight announcement. Will passengers for Pan American Flight 313 for New York please proceed to departure gate 12. Gate 12 for Flight 313 for New York. Thank you. (*ting tong*).

Immediately:

(*ting tong*). Staff announcement. Will Mr Ramesh Desai and Mrs Sukhdev Kaur report at once to the catering managers' office. Flight announcement. Will passengers for British Airways Flight 308 for Johannesburg please proceed to departure gate 17. Gate 17 for passengers to Johannesburg. This is your final call. Thank you. (*ting tong.*)

Lights down a little on Pakistani. Lights on JOWETT *and* DAWSON, *round a table, at a meeting. It is clear that there are others present.* JOWETT *has the report open in front of him.*

JOWETT. Right, brothers and, sister. I hope you've had a chance to cast your eyes across the oracle. I think it's general conclusions are what we'd have thought. We are, for instance . . . um . . . 'sometimes unmindful of our overall responsibility . . .' um, 'unwise counsel . . . poor communications that perhaps could have been . . .' cetera etcetera, 'misjudgement rather than a conscious ill-intention'. I should point out that the strike committee is accused of being irresponsible, and outside militants, and all that kind of thing. As far as what's been recommended . . . We are told, as if we didn't know, that, um . . . 'unions have tended to resist overt outside interference in their affairs . . .' and we're left with, shall we say, a rather vague exhortation to see that everyone is represented equally.

Slight pause.

To which we shall genuinely respond.

Pause.

So. All in all, I think we've come through this quite well. Any comments?

Pause. DAWSON *raises her hand.*

Yes, Joan?

DAWSON. Well, I just wondered, George . . .

Slight pause.

When you say, we've come through this, I just wondered . . .

Slight pause. Change of tack:

What you mean by, 'genuinely respond'?

Lights off DAWSON *and* JOWETT. *Lights up again on the Pakistani.*

LOUDSPEAKER (*ting tong*). Staff announcement. Will Ramesh Desai or Mrs Sukhdev Kaur or any other members of the Terminal Three Catering Division please report without delay to the catering manager's office. Repeat, any members of the Catering Division report to the catering manager's office without delay. (*ting tong.*)

Lights fade a little on Pakistani. Lights on WATTS, HUSSEIN *and* BHANDARI, *who are also discussing the report.*

WATTS. Well. I think the first thing to say is that in general this is excellent. It accepts almost all our arguments. Although it does make predictable remarks about irresponsible advice and so on, it is much more critical of the other parties than of you.

HUSSEIN. Specifically?

WATTS. Well, there's a problem. You see, she recommends that the choice of which workers are or aren't to be retained during the redundancy should be made on the basis of merit and experience, regardless of race colour creed etcetera. The problem is the word experience. Because, the legacy, what's happened in the past, has brought about a situation in which the Asian workers are, in general, inexperienced on Sultzer looms. So, in effect, what's bound to happen is, the whites will get first pick. And the only way to stop that would be some kind of quota system, which –

BHANDARI. Which is illegal.

WATTS. Yes. It's not her fault, of course. Law of the land.

HUSSEIN. Of course. The law of the land.

Lights off WATTS, BHANDARI *and* HUSSEIN. *Lights back up on the Pakistani.*

LOUDSPEAKER (*ting tong*). Flight announcement. Will passengers for Air Pakistan Flight 321 for Karachi please proceed to Departure Gate 19. Gate 19, Air Pakistan Flight for Karachi. Thank you. (*ting tong.*)

An immigration OFFICIAL *stands by the Pakistani. He consults his clipboard.*

OFFICIAL. Kadir?

The Pakistani looks up.

Abdul Kadir?

The Pakistani nods. The OFFICIAL *nods towards the loudspeaker.*

Your flight. It's time to go.

The Pakistani puts the report down on the next chair. He stands and picks up his hand baggage. The OFFICIAL *picks up the report and glances at it. Then tossing the report on the chair.*

OFFICIAL. OK, Kadir. Wave goodbye to England. Sorry, can't be au revoir.

They are about to go when the LOUDSPEAKER *intervenes.*

LOUDSPEAKER (*ting tong*). Ladies and gentlemen, this is a special announcement to all passengers. We regret to announce that due to unofficial industrial action by catering staff, all Terminal Three refreshment facilities are temporarily suspended. We apologise to all passengers for any inconvenience caused. Thank you. (*ting tong.*)

OFFICIAL. Bloody hell. Ask me mate, you're well out of it.

ABDUL KADIR *smiles. He stubs out his cigarette.*

ABDUL KADIR. OK. Let's go.

Scene Twenty-Five

The stage.
The company.

1ST PERFORMER. What you have just seen is a piece of fiction. There was no such place as Beckley, no such union as the National Union of Weavers, and no such firm as Darley Park Mills. None of the characters are real.

2ND PERFORMER. However, most of the events described in the play are based on things that have really happened, in different industrial disputes, in different places, at different times.

3RD PERFORMER. At a firm in Nottingham called Crepe Sizes, for instance, Asian workers founded a TGWU branch. When five workers were sacked, the Asians came out on strike, but their white colleagues remained at work.

4TH PERFORMER. At Standard Telephones in North London, white workers refused to train a West Indian machine setter. The AUEW made the consequent strike official, but allowed its white members to work normally.

5TH PERFORMER. At British Celanese, a plastics factory in Derby, the union took four months to recognise the credentials of an elected Asian shop steward. In eighteen months, he saw the works convenor once.

6TH PERFORMER. At Harword Cash Mills, Mansfield, the Race Relations Board ruled that there was no discrimination when Asian workers were paid the same wages for a compulsory 60-hour-week as white workers were paid for 48.

7TH PERFORMER. During a strike by Asian workers at Imperial Typewriters, Leicester, the National Front organised a march in which many white workers participated. In their journal Spearhead, the Front described the white workers' actions as a racial struggle against both communism and international capitalism. A year later, the American owners of the firm closed down their Hull and Leicester factories. At Hull there was an occupation, but at Leicester, the divided workforce just caved in.

8TH PERFORMER. At Mansfield Hosiery Mills, Loughborough, the National Front was also active during an Asian strike against discrimination in promotion to high-paid knitters' posts. During the strike, the white knitters accepted a productivity and redundancy agreement that they had previously rejected, and the company appointed a number of white knitters brought in from outside. During a subsequent Court of Inquiry, it emerged that the company had entered into a covert agreement with the knitters not to promote black workers.

1ST PERFORMER. After the Inquiry, the Hosiery Workers' Union President commented: 'We helped the Asians far more than we helped our own people. This is what stuck in my craw all the time we were trying to get a settlement'.

2ND PERFORMER. It all depends on who are whose own people.

Chronology of the Dispute at Darley Park Mills Ltd, Beckley, summer 1975.

April
Mon 21: After a series of unsatisfactory meetings with senior steward Frank Kitchen, Asian nightshift workers write to the General Secretary of the National Union of Weavers, George Jowett, to press their demands for an improvement on the nightshift bonus and the piecework rates on the old (Dobcross) looms.

Wed 23: Hameed Faruqi, nightshift shop steward, complains to the Race Relations Board about the fact that Asians at the Mill are forced to do overtime on the nightshift.

Thurs 24: Following the receipt of the letter to Mr Jowett, Frank Kitchen meets the Asians to discuss their grievances.

Mon 28: A further meeting is held between Mr Kitchen and the Asians, with George Jowett in attendance. A case is drawn up.

Tues 29: The union writes to management, presenting the case of the nightshift workers.

May
Mon 5: Mr Jowett and Mr Kitchen meet management and present the Asians' case. Management turns down the demands.

Wed 7: Mr Jowett and Mr Kitchen meet the Asian workers and report back on the meeting with management. The Asians ask that seven days' strike notice be given.

Thurs 8: The union writes to management informing them of the Asians' reaction.

Thurs 15: The Asian workers meet Mr Kitchen and enquire about progress on the claim. Mr Kitchen informs them there has been no progress, and the Asians tell him they are going to take strike action. Mr Kitchen advises them to delay until they have seen Mr Jowett.

Fri 16: At a meeting with the Asians, Mr Jowett advises them not to strike. However, the Asians set up their own strike committee and come out on strike.

Thurs 22: Mrs Anshuya Ridley of the Manchester Community Relations Council is called in to assist in resolving the dispute. She has a preliminary meeting with the union and management.

Fri 23: Violence flares on the picket line and two arrests of

Asian strikers are made.

Tues 27:   After a second meeting involving Mrs Ridley, proposals for a return to work are agreed. That evening, the terms are put to the strikers and accepted.

Wed 28:   On their return, the Asians find that two white time-weavers have been appointed on the old loom (Dobcross) dayshift, in apparent breach of the Ridley agreement. That evening, the strikers meet and decide to resume strike action.

Thur 29:   The strike restarts.

June

Wed 4:   The management sends letters to all strikers giving seven days' notice of termination of their contracts of employment.

Thurs 5:   The management issues a new scheme for phasing out almost all the Dobcross looms and for a transfer to a three-shift operation on new weaving machines (Sultzers).

Wed 11:   The strikers are dismissed from employment by the company.

Fri 13:   A delegation of strikers meets George Jowett to demand that the strike be made official.

Mon 16:   The union executive meets and makes the strike official.

Tues 17:   The Race Relations Board makes its report on Mr Faruqi's complaint of discrimination.

Wed 18:   The non-striking workers meet to discuss the management's new scheme for a transfer to the Sultzer weaving machines. Against Mr Jowett's advice, the workers accept the scheme.

Thurs 19:   The union meets management to attempt to secure an agreement to end the strike. Management refuses to guarantee that no redundancies among the Asian strikers will take place.

Fri 20:   The strikers meet and reject the terms for a return to work, demanding a 'no victimization' clause.

Mon 23:   Violence again flares on the picket line and fifteen arrests are made.

Thurs 26:   Further violence and more arrests on the picket line. The Secretary of State for Employment sets up a Court of Inquiry to consider the case.